How to Establish a Jail and Prison Ministry

How to Establish a Jail and Prison Ministry

DUANE PEDERSON

Foreword by Corrie ten Boom

Thomas Nelson Publishers
Nashville

Library of Congress Cataloging in Publication Data

Pederson, Duane.
How to establish a jail and prison ministry.

1. Church work with prisoners. I. Title.
BV4465.P4 253.7'5 78-27438
ISBN 0-8407-5675-5

To the many men and women I have met in prison during the past years.

For your understanding and love shown to me . . . an outsider.

May Almighty God continue to bless and protect you and your family while you are apart from each other.

Contents

Acknowledgments

A special thank you to these friends who through their support, encouragement, and vital input helped make this manual a reality:

Bobb and Cheryl Biehl
Corrie ten Boom
Bill and Bettie Butler
Chaplain Manford and Jeanette Craig
Ed and Thelma Elfstrom
Chaplain Harry and Kay Howard
Chaplain Larry and Blanch Mathre
Bill Needham
Chaplain General J. A. Nichels
Pamela Rosewell
Chaplain Don and Phyllis Severson
Chaplain Frederick and Doris Silber
Chaplain Ed and Zel Stelle
Chaplain Phil and Carol Wagner
Dr. Jackson and Margie Wilcox

Foreword

This book is one of the results of a vision the Lord gave me. Some time ago I had heart trouble and had to choose between going to heaven or having a "pacemaker." Although my longing was to be in heaven, the Lord made it clear that there was still work for me to do here. Coming from the operating room, I asked the Lord why He had given me back my life. His answer was very clear: "There is an important work to do. Bring people who work in prisons together and train volunteers to work in prisons and jails, particularly in those places where the gospel is not being brought." As a result of this vision, the Association of Christian Prison Workers came into being, with Duane Pederson as its president.

I have been in prison. I knew the agony of being away from the people I loved, the dark, lonely nights spent in a place where the door could only be opened from the outside. Without the Lord I would never have made it through those hard times. He preserved me because He had work for me to do. But I know there are thousands of prisoners today who have no hope. They spend their lives behind bars, growing bitter and feeling hopelessly lost. They need Jesus. You have in your hands a book that contains much practical advice. It tells you not only *how* to take the gospel to prisoners, but *why* it must be done.

The author of this book has many years of experience in working with prisoners. Duane is a man who knows and loves prisoners and who is himself a prisoner of the Lord Jesus Christ.

One day Jesus Christ will say to you, "I was in prison and you visited me" or "You did not visit me." Give room to the Holy Spirit as you read this book, and He will teach you your part in the vital work of taking the gospel to some of the most wounded men and women in the world—prisoners.

Corrie ten Boom
August, 1978

Preface

"Don't make promises you can't keep." "Be yourself." "Be a friend." These are some extremely fundamental principles of working in prisons—and of writing a book such as this one.

Don't make promises you can't keep. I can't promise that if you know nothing about prison or jail ministry when you start this book that you will be a totally qualified, fully trained prison volunteer when you finish. That may be a promise you would like to hear me make: "Presto, you are qualified." Unfortunately, this book is only a beginning point.

I can promise that you will learn some of the most basic information and "how-to's" that a panel of highly qualified chaplains and myself could present to you.

I can promise you this book doesn't contain a lot of unproven ideas; rather, there are practical suggestions proven hundreds of times.

Be yourself. A prisoner doesn't need a theologian or someone with a Ph.D. to explain every "jot and tittle" of Hebrew transcript . . . he needs a Christian friend who can be himself. Although many will think of you as a Christian prison volunteer, think of yourself by your first name. "Tom is going to talk to Joe inside" or "Mary is going to talk to Suzy inside." No titles, no pretense of "super-Christian," no "holier-than-thou" attitude. Go as though you were meeting a friend for coffee at the local restaurant. Let your love, and God's love through you, love each person.

I certainly don't have all the answers to prison work. Who can say he has all the answers but a fool? In this book I am just myself, Duane, sharing with you the things I've found that work time and again.

Be a friend. Part of being a friend is just helping a person through "hard times" or helping someone deal with things he may never have faced before. A friend can help someone "see the light at the end of the tunnel."

How I wish when I first started working "inside" I had had a book like this. I have tried to look at you, the reader, as a close friend of mine who is interested in prison work but hasn't yet been inside. I've tried to help you know what to do . . . what not to do . . . who to see . . . where to go . . . and why these things are important.

I would like to thank all the friends both outside and inside who have taught me not to make promises I couldn't keep, who have been their honest selves with me, who have let me see their hurts and tears, and who have been Christian friends to me.

All royalties from the sale of this book are assigned to Christian Prison Volunteers for furthering formalized training seminars to qualify people to work in prisons. For information on the seminars, or if I can be of any help to you personally, please write to me in care of Christian Prison Volunteers, Box 1949, Hollywood, CA 90028.

Duane Pederson
November, 1978

1

Prison Ministries: Today's Desperate Need

The scene is familiar. Siren whining, the patrol car swerves around the corner, screeches to a stop, and two uniformed policemen leap out to chase a suspect. They catch him, put him into the patrol car, and drive him to the police station. He is fingerprinted and "booked." Scene fades, commercial appears, and another television show has ended. The police have done their work; law and order have been reestablished.

But what happened to that person after he or she was arrested? Where did they go? The TV dramas rarely take us down the narrow corridors between the barred cells to show us what became of the person so dramatically arrested. We usually stop at the front desk of the jail or the gates of the prison. On television and in real life, we see only the beginning of a story; we rarely know its ending. But what *is* the story? What happened to that person who disappeared into a jail or prison? And what difference should that make to those people on the "outside" who claim the name of Christ, the One who spoke of setting the prisoners free?

A HIDDEN SOCIETY

If you are like most people, you know very little about the prisons and jails of America. Yet this ignorance is the greatest barrier to seeing and meeting the desperate emotional and spiritual needs that exist among the millions of people affected each year by the criminal justice system of our country.

Lest you hastily say, "They deserve it," or "It's too unpleasant; I don't want to think about it," please remember that we are not speaking of inanimate objects, but of human beings—men and women who love and cry and fear and hope. They too have been made in the image of their Creator. They, too, can come into a new and vital relationship with Jesus Christ as Lord and Savior. If you say these people are guilty of crimes and deserve to be punished, remember also that from God's perspective we are all guilty and condemned for our sins—regardless of how we view their severity. But from the same perspective, there is a way to establish a proper relationship with God and with society. You can be the one to bring that news to people in prisons and jails who would like to know what true caring, love, and friendship really are.

The men and women behind bars are part of one of the largest systems in our society. America's criminal justice system costs about fifteen billion dollars a year; it employs the equivalent of a million people full time, making it one of the largest government programs in existence. These costs are not spent by some distant government body; the largest share of the money is spent at the *local* level by your city or county, and that is where two-thirds of the people are employed.[1]

Accurate statistics are difficult to find, but the American Correctional Association estimates that there are approximately 6,000 correctional facilities of all types in this country, from minimum-security work camps to high-walled prisons. A 1974 survey by the Law Enforcement Assistance Administration (LEAA) reported 608 state-operated and 47 federal prison institutions, and new ones have been built since that survey. At city and county levels, the LEAA study revealed almost 4,000 local jails, but because that survey excluded almost 9,700 of the smallest communities, most people believe the number of jails (and their inmates) was greatly undercounted.[2] Attorney Ronald Goldfarb, author of several studies of the U.S. correctional system, estimates that the actual number of local (city and county) jails in this country is well over 5,000.[3]

The diversity is in more than numbers. In addition to federal and state prisons and local jails, there are work release centers, halfway houses, road camps, work farms, juvenile detention halls, reformatories, prison reception centers, prison hospitals, and a variety of other confinement facilities.

Although these facilities are for confinement, each has a different emphasis. A work release center allows an inmate to hold a job in the community during the day and return to the center for confinement at night. Halfway houses may be for persons who have been released on parole or who have completed a sentence. They can stay at the house while seeking employment and a permanent place to live. Road camps, often located in rural areas, house inmates who do maintenance on roads and highways. Work farms provide farm-type employment for inmates, often including the production of food for other prisons.

Detention halls are typically found in cities and are places where juveniles can be held separately from adult prisoners. Reformatories are for juveniles who have been convicted of a crime and sentenced. Reception centers are types of prisons designed to receive and orient newly convicted persons. Prison hospitals are built for security so that seriously ill prisoners may receive medical attention but still be confined.

A single community may have several types of confinement institutions. Tallahassee, Florida, a medium-sized city, has a county jail, a federal correctional institution (medium-security prison), a state road camp, a work release center, and a halfway house for adults. For juvenile offenders there are two halfway houses (one for boys, the other for girls), a detention center, and a state facility for drug abuse offenders. Larger cities may have many different kinds of facilities, and even small communities may have more than just a jail.

A SIZABLE SOCIETY

So much for the buildings; what of the people in them? In 1977, state and federal prisons held 275,500 persons; ten percent of these were in federal custody, while the rest were held by the state prison systems.[4] The number of people confined in prisons *and* jails at any one time is between 400,000 and 500,000. That's the equivalent population of a city the size of Denver or Atlanta, or of the entire state of Vermont.[5]

A half million people in confinement is a sobering total. Equally sobering is the fact that the ratio of inmates per 100,000 citizens in the United States is the highest of any democratic nation. Prison population is at an all-time high. The increase in inmates from 1976 to 1977 was the largest ever recorded in a single year, and researchers predict that prison populations will continue to increase through 1985.[6]

Even these statistics don't reveal the full impact of the penal system. City and county jails touch the lives of more people than any other correctional institution. Hans W. Mattick, co-director of the Center for Studies in Criminal Justice at the University of Chicago Law School, writes: "The actual number of persons passing through America's jails in a year is at least one million and may be as high as four million men, women, and children. This is the population equivalent of a very large city or a medium-sized state and is at least four times the number who annually pass through state and federal prisons combined."[7] His estimate of the number of persons affected by jails each year is about three million.

Three million men, women—and children.

The Juvenile Tragedy

Are you surprised that there are children in jails? One of the tragedies of our society is that there are often so few alternatives to imprisonment. The National Council on Crime and Delinquency estimated in 1966 that 100,000 children, ages seven to seventeen, were detained in county jails and police lockups every year. In many cases there are no separate facilities for juveniles and they are kept with adults.

During the same year, another 400,000 juveniles were held in detention centers. More than 10 percent of the children in these centers were under twelve. Most had had no trials; many were not even accused of a crime. They were simply neglected and rejected, or there was no place else for them to go.[8] Some were runaways; others were "throwaways," rejected by their families and told to leave home. A government-sponsored study estimates that in 1975 about 70,000 children were "thrown away" in this country—and the actual total may be much higher. Many of these "throwaway" children end up in jail.

Jimmy is typical of such rejected young people. He was fourteen when he finally left home. He came from an upper-middle-class family in the Midwest, but the affluence couldn't make up for the turmoil of a broken home. His parents could no longer stand each other and Jimmy felt he, too, was no longer welcome.

I met Jimmy on the streets of Los Angeles where he had been surviving by selling homosexual favors. Jimmy appeared to be easygoing and happy, but inside he was torn apart. He told me how he had tried to go back to his parents. Once, after being picked up by the police, Jimmy gave them his father's name and telephone number. They called and asked Jimmy's father if he had a son fitting Jimmy's description.

"No," said Jimmy's father.

"But sir, this boy says he's your son."

Came the harsh reply, "If you've got him, you can keep him."

Total rejection—and no place to go but jail.

Warren was only fifteen when we first met. He too had been living on the streets. His mother didn't want him and he had sought out his stepfather. A meeting was arranged but the stepfather never came. A week later Warren was in jail for auto theft. If that father had only cared, a young boy could have been spared a prison record.

Those on the Outside

But not all offenders are in jail or prison. Each year there is a large turnover in the prison and jail populations; many thousands of inmates are conditionally released and new offenders come into custody. The President's Commission on Law Enforcement and Administration of Justice reported in 1967 that about two-thirds of the offender population were on parole or probation; one-third were in confinement.

And for every prisoner there are perhaps three to five other persons who are affected. Wives, husbands, children, brothers, sisters, in-laws, friends—all these can be affected by the prison experience of one person. If three million people each year directly experience the trauma of imprisonment, then perhaps nine to fifteen million more are influenced through their relationship to the one behind bars.

A SOCIETY THAT NEEDS GOD

The statistics may seem as cold and impersonal as the gray stone walls and steel bars of a prison cell, but every statistic is a living human being, someone who started out with great potential and then somehow went wrong. But that potential remains. Said one inmate at California's San Quentin prison, "Though we have broken the rules, we're still human. We still breathe and eat and love."[9] It is to these people that the church is called and commanded to minister.

Most inmates have great emotional, psychological, and spiritual need. They live with the constant threat of violence. They feel lonely, humiliated, angry, and apprehensive. They have little success or encouragement in life and few good examples to look to. Many need counseling to help them understand who they are and how they can relate successfully to other people. And most inmates need to hear of the grace and love of God and accept the healing of their persons and the establishment of a proper relationship to God through Jesus Christ. Without this, even the best prison experience will be of no ultimate value.

There is a desperate and overwhelming need in our prisons and jails today for a clear communication of the Word of divine grace and compassion as seen in the lives of faithful Christians. You should know that chaplains are but a faithful few, working against great odds. There are only about 400 to 600 full-time prison chaplains, most of them in state and federal prisons. The rest are divided among jails and juvenile instutitions.[10] A typical prison of 2,000 inmates may have only two full-time chaplains, sometimes assisted by local pastors working part time or by volunteers. A study of state adult penal institutions in the mid-1960s revealed a ratio of one chaplain to every 560 inmates, and that ratio has not changed much.[11]

A typical prison may have more people than the average parish or church congregation, and a chaplain has more than a full-time job leading worship services and religious education classes, counseling, coordinating volunteers (if he has any), providing a link with the local community, and acting as the manager or administrator of the institution's entire religious program.

Said one chaplain, "As a rule of thumb, a chaplain might work in depth with perhaps one hundred men during a year, and he might see several hundred others to a much lesser extent; and that's out of a prison population of two thousand, with a turnover of perhaps a thousand men a year." Almost no chaplain has any full-time staff assistance; at best, there is an inmate clerk. There is no way, therefore, that a chaplain can minister to the needs of more than a small portion of the inmates at his institution.

No Shepherds for the Sheep

The sad fact is that some prisons and most jails *have no chaplains and many have no religious services at all.* The 1972 LEAA survey (referred to earlier) revealed that 42 percent of local jails had no religious services of any kind. That is about 1,600 jails, at least a dozen of them large (250 or more inmates). When you recall that this survey undercounted local jails, the actual number of jails without religious services may be well over 2,000.

A 1974 survey of state prisons showed that almost all of them provided for religious worship. Nevertheless, 4 percent, or several dozen institutions, had no such services.[12] Since attendance is voluntary and only a minority of inmates take part, the fact that religious services are provided is no indication of the extent to which the spiritual needs of the inmates are being met. Chaplains know they can't wait for inmates to come to the chapel.

Chaplain Harry Howard of San Quentin visits cell-to-cell when inmates are "locked down" or confined to their cells. They don't have the freedom to walk about the yard or to go any place else in the prison, so Chaplain Howard comes to the men where they are—talking, counseling, providing literature, and doing what he can to show the love of Christ to people whose whole world is a concrete barred cell.

Not only do many jails have no religious services, but of those that do, the majority depend upon outside groups to provide these services. This is particularly true for the small jails, but it is also the case for about 40 percent of the large jails. Clearly, the burden of a Christian witness in jails and prisons falls to the churches and committed lay people of each community. If they do nothing, the saving, healing, comforting Word of God will not reach those behind bars.

In one sense, prisons and jails are not being ignored. Hundreds of humanitarian and special-interest groups are actively working on different aspects of corrections: prison reform, offender rehabilitation, legal needs, employment for ex-offenders, juvenile counseling, and prison libraries—to name just a few. Depending heavily upon volunteers, these various programs are caring for, counseling, teaching, or sponsoring inmates and former inmates. Volunteers are able to help reduce the number of recidivists (repeat offenders), encourage inmates to develop a better self-image, provide for alternatives to imprisonment, and make the correctional system more humane in general.

What's more, these volunteer efforts are often effective. One study of more than 250 reports on prison volunteer programs concluded that volunteers were found "to be at least as effective in accomplishing their objectives . . . as formal methods of rehabilitating offenders."[13] Most of this activity, however, focuses on prisons, not jails, and the actual number of people who are in direct and continuing contact with inmates is very, very small. Furthermore, only a small portion of these are engaged in spiritual ministries.

Where are the Christians, the faithful witnesses and commissioned ambassadors of Jesus Christ, the men and women with a spiritual distinction who can honestly share their faith with others? The chaplain can't do it all. There are many thousands of prisoners who will respond when approached with understanding and genuine concern. We need Christian men and women who can communicate love, compassion, and a clear testimony to people not normally exposed to the Christian faith.

A SOCIETY WITHOUT HOPE?

I recognize that some inmates must remain confined for their own good as well as for the protection of society. But are we to forget that they are still human beings? And most other prisoners will eventually be released back into society after serving their sentences. What will they have experienced during their confinement that will encourage them to make a successful transition? For people in both categories, an encounter with the grace of God through Jesus Christ can be an utterly transforming experience. As Christians, you and I have the opportunity to be channels of that grace, as God permits us and as we allow it to happen.

Let's not be hesitant or fearful. Instead, let's use every opportunity to be such channels. As Paul urged Timothy, "Preach the Word of God urgently at all times, whenever you get the chance . . . when it is convenient and when it is not" (2 Tim.4:2, TLB). No one is beyond God's reach. That is the hope that should encourage us as we seek to minister to those in prisons and jails.

How God Helped a Prisoner "Beat" Alcatraz

Rev. Paul Markstrom gives a vivid illustration of how God can work in the lives of prisoners who seem beyond changing. He tells of James V. Bennett, former director of the U.S. Bureau of Prisons, speaking to a group of federal chaplains and saying, "I have many testimonials in my files of the value of Christian teaching, but none has come to my attention recently that is more vivid or more realistic than that of a prisoner who wrote an article for publication which he called 'Escape From Alcatraz.' The young author had been rejected by his parents at the age of fifteen and pushed from one orphanage or institution to another. Feeling unwanted and bitter, he reacted by trying to square his account with society by committing one crime after another in a career which finally culminated in a spectacular bank robbery. He was caught and committed to Atlanta [U.S. federal penitentiary] where he spent his time—by his own admission—thinking of ways to escape. He spent every waking moment trying to find some weakness in the prison and he finally found one."

Mr. Bennett recounted how the young man managed to wriggle through a storm sewer that led from the prison yard to beyond the walls. After seven or eight hours of struggling through the narrow pipe and forcing aside the barriers with a wrench, the man was free—only to be caught soon after and returned to prison. He became so discouraged that he actually developed a psychosis and was transferred to the prison at Alcatraz.

Continued Mr. Bennett, "There, under the influence of the chaplain and his religious reading, he learned that he could, as he phrased it, 'beat Alcatraz.' He beat it, he said, by concluding that before he went down for the third time in the sea of misery, he would try to reach toward God. He acknowledged that when he offered himself, he wasn't offering much but what he was he offered freely and wholly. This is how he described what happened: 'And God took me up. He took me—confused, searching, worthless me. Why He accepted me I don't know. I'm afraid even to ask the question. Somehow it must be explained in terms of love. But just how could God love me? I didn't know then, and I don't know now. All I know is that I surrendered every last bit of myself and He took me at my word. Ever since that wonderful moment, I have had the peace that comes only from Him. God came to me and has remained with me.

'All of this may shound like nonsense. I don't know how the good psychologist would explain it all. All I know is that I have escaped from myself and found my God. And so for me prison has lost its sting . . . I dare to say, Lord, remember me. And now my cross is a labor of love. I have escaped from the two worlds by finding their meaning in yet a third world—the city of God.' This man, you will be happy to know, was eventually returned to Atlanta and not long afterwards, paroled."[14]

This young man saw his utter helplessness before God and realized he could do nothing to bring himself to God. But God could accept him because Jesus Christ had paid the penalty for that man's sins, and the Holy Spirit performed a work of regeneration and renewal in his heart. Truly, as Jesus said, "With men this is impossible, but with God all things are possible" (Matt. 19:26, RSV).

The committed Christian volunteer has a vital role to play in today's correctional system. It is a unique and demanding ministry with its share of frustrations and disappointments, but the rewards far outweigh them. Jesus was specifically including prisoners when He said, "Truly, I say to you, as you did it to one of the least of these my brethren, you did it to me" (Matt. 25:40, RSV).

CHAPTER 1 REVIEW QUESTIONS

1. In terms of dollars spent, the U.S. criminal justice system is
   a) a relatively small governmental program.
   b) about average in size.
   c) one of the largest governmental programs.

2. Most money for jails and prisons is spent at the
   a) federal government level.
   b) state government level.
   c) local government level.

3. The number of jails in the United States is
   a) more than 10,000.
   b) about 8,700.
   c) between 4,000 and 5,000.

4. The number of people held in state and federal prisons is
   a) about 125,000.
   b) about 275,000.
   c) more than one million.

5. The number of persons in prison in recent years has
   a) remained about the same.
   b) increased fairly rapidly.
   c) slowly decreased.

6. All persons in jail have been tried and convicted of some crime.
   a) True.
   b) False.

7. Most jails have full-time or volunteer chaplains.
   a) True.
   b) False.

8. Many jails have no religious services for inmates.
   a) True.
   b) False.

9. Volunteers are needed in prisons because prison chaplains cannot provide all the needed spiritual ministries.
   a) True.
   b) False.

10. People in jails and prisons deserve to be there.
    a) I strongly agree.
    b) I agree somewhat.
    c) I disagree somewhat.
    d) I strongly disagree.

2

The Scriptural Mandate for Prison Ministries

Jesus is in San Quentin. Jesus is in Leavenworth. Jesus is in Attica and Danbury and Sing Sing. He's in your local city or county jail. How do I know? Because He said so.

Someday the righteous will ask of the King, " 'When did we ever see you sick or in prison, and visit you?' The King will reply, 'I tell you, whenever you did this for one of the least important of these brothers of mine, you did it for me!' " (Matt. 25:39,40, TEV).

When was the last time *you* visited Jesus in prison?

"I don't want to get involved" seems to be the unspoken motto of too many Christians. On every side there are the cries of those who hurt and the claims of those who seek justice. Yet so often Christians close their ears and turn away their eyes. We evade and avoid because to see and to hear would be painful and our consciences might demand action. To know a need exists and to do nothing is to be calloused, indifferent, and unloving—hardly what Jesus commanded of His followers.

THE CHRISTIAN IN PRISON

Nowhere is the contrast of belief versus action so evident as in ministering to people in jails and prisons. On the one hand, Christians have long been concerned for those in prison. Onesiphorus could probably be called the "patron saint" of prison visitation, as Paul writes lovingly of his visits while Paul was imprisoned in Rome (2 Tim. 1:16).

In the United States as early as 1787, the Quakers of Philadelphia were providing religious instruction and counseling for jail inmates. James V. Bennett, former director of the U.S. Bureau of Prisons, once told a meeting of correctional officials, "All through the history of punishment runs the curious fact that practically the only people displaying a genuine interest in the criminals' lot are those driven by the spirit of religious mission."

On the other hand, of the tens of millions of active Christians in the United States, only a very small number are involved in ministries to prisoners (despite the fact that jails are found in almost every community that also has a church). The opportunities are many and near at hand, yet churches and individual Christians have often not responded. Could it be that Christians feel awkward or uncomfortable about showing love to those behind bars?

Of all people, Christians should be familiar with the needs and experiences of prisoners. Throughout the Bible we read examples, descriptions, and commandments about prisons, prisoners, bondage, captivity, and slavery. The Bible mentions prison, prisoners, or imprisonment more than 130 times. For various reasons many of the "heroes of the faith" ended up with "prison records." Joseph spent at least two years in prison, falsely accused of attempted rape (Genesis 39). Samson was imprisoned by the Philistines (Judges 16). Jeremiah was put into King Zedekiah's dungeon twice, once for unpopular preaching and once when falsely accused of treason (Jeremiah 32, 37). Many of the apostles were thrown into prison by the Sadducees (Acts 5), while Herod imprisoned not only Paul, but John the Baptist (Matthew 4) and Peter (Acts 12). The apostle Paul had a lengthy prison record; he served sentences at Fortress Antonia in Jerusalem (Acts 23), at Herod's castle in Caesarea (Acts 23), in a local jail in Philippi (Acts 16), and probably two different times in a prison in Rome.

Christians both notable and unknown have been imprisoned throughout church history, from the time of Rome to the era of Mao tse-tung. John Bunyan and Dietrich Bonhoeffer are but two of many famous Christians who saw prison walls from the inside, while modern China, Russia, and Uganda have seen thousands of Christian martyrs known only to God. Indeed, Jesus said that being a faithful Christian may lead to prison. He warned His disciples that they faced arrest when He sent them out as "sheep to wolves" (Matthew 10) and again, before His return, he warned that believers would also face imprisonment (Matthew 24). Conversely, being a prisoner may also lead to faith, as one thief discovered on Calvary.

THE SCRIPTURAL MANDATE

Obviously, in most of the above instances, the individuals were imprisoned because of their faith—not because they had broken the state's criminal code by being thieves or murderers. But as Christians we are to care for those in prison—regardless of how they came to be there—because *Christ specifically commands us to do so.* First of all, ministering to prisoners is part of His general commandment to witness to *all* persons *everywhere.* Jesus spoke to Jews and Samaritans, to religious leaders and poor fishermen, to the rich and to the outcasts. The Great Commission of Matthew 28 urges us to go into all the world to disciple, baptize, and teach, and the commission is reinforced by the words of our risen Lord to His disciples in Acts 1:8.

Jesus specifically refers to those in prison (Matthew 25) and indicates that caring for them is one way—along with helping the sick, the hungry, the lonely, and the unclothed—to minister to Him. In the Matthew account those who have visited and ministered to prisoners are blessed; those who have not are rejected. This is an obligation that cannot be ignored.

The New Testament says that Christians are to be ministers,

witnesses, ambassadors, and servants—all titles of activity and purpose. After we are saved, our gratitude for God's mercy should prompt us to show, abundantly, the same mercy and kindness to others. God expects us to perform good deeds and they will be evaluated; that's why we are created, writes Paul to the Ephesian church (Eph. 2:10). Paul reminds the Christians at Rome that each person has certain abilities that are to be used to benefit others (Rom. 12:6–8). Jesus did this for us; should we not do likewise for others—for prisoners? "Remember those who are in prison, as though in prison with them," says the writer to the Hebrews (Heb. 13:3, RSV).

Beyond Christ's commands is the simple fact that God's grace can reach to all people. No one is beyond hope. God is not willing that any (including prisoners) should perish (2 Pet. 3:9); He wants all to know the truth (1 Tim. 2:4). John Newton, the famous English slave trader turned preacher, described his experience with the outreach of God's love in his well-known hymn "Amazing Grace." He wrote of the grace that could save a "wretch like me." For his epitaph Newton wrote, "John Newton, clerk, once an infidel and libertine, a servant of slaves in Africa, was by the mercy of our Lord and Saviour Jesus Christ preserved, restored, pardoned, and appointed to preach the faith he had so long labored to destroy."

Paul points to himself as the great example of how God's grace can change even the worst of sinners. He described himself as having spoken evil of God, persecuting and insulting Him, and of being the worst of sinners, "but God was merciful to me in order that Christ Jesus might show his full patience in dealing with me, the worst of sinners, as an example for all those who would later believe in him and receive eternal life" (1 Tim. 1.16, TEV).

Four crimes account for the majority of prison inmates: robbery, burglary, homicide, and narcotics violations. Are men and women guilty of these crimes somehow beyond God's grace? Is there no way they can truly hear and respond to the wonderful message of salvation through Jesus Christ? Such certainly can and do when faithful Christians show the love and compassion Jesus commanded of His followers.

Evangelist Ralph Bell had conducted crusades in numerous prisons around the nation as a member of the Billy Graham evangelistic team. When asked about what evidence he had seen of the impact and response of the gospel in prisons, evangelist Bell said, "I've been excited about the tremendous hunger I've seen among inmates, both men and women. A lot of people who have been in and out of prison have grown weary with that kind of life, and they want something better. Others are first-timers, and they don't want any part of that life any longer. Many are hungry and waiting for an opportunity to meet Christ."[1]

Rev. Manford Craig, Protestant chaplain at the federal penitentiary at Leavenworth, said, "There are many fine men who have been converted since entering the penitentiary, and there's a tremendous satisfaction in seeing them develop and mature in their spiritual lives. I've seen broken homes reunited. I know men who have left prison and become ordained ministers and are now successful pastors. These things do happen, and they remind us that our labor is not in vain in the Lord."[2]

GOD DOESN'T MAKE JUNK!

What does the gospel of Jesus Christ have to offer men and women who have seen little in their lives except rejection, failure, and unhappiness? They are offered forgiveness and pardon, a chance to truly say, "I'm sorry." That's a new experience for many of them. Judgment and condemnation they know very well—not forgiveness. For others, the important message is acceptance—acceptance of themselves by Christ and by others. They have a chance to see self-worth and gain a sense of personal dignity. As someone has said, "God doesn't make junk." Many prisoners have seen themselves as only junk, and it's a great feeling for them to realize God didn't make them that way nor does He want them to be that way.

Still other inmates respond to the fundamental Christian

themes of love, hope, and peace (with themselves, with others, and with God). These people are faced with an entirely new set of values and perspectives that they have never dared to consider before. Christianity provides a way for them to be rid of the guilt many of them feel, not only guilt for crimes (sins), but for having disappointed others—parents, wives, children, and friends. The Bible plainly shows that at the Cross, God laid upon Jesus the guilt of the whole world. For our sake, God "made him to be sin who knew no sin, so that in him we might become the righteousness of God" (2 Cor. 5:21, RSV).

Prisoners also learn how they can cope with the pressures and problems around them. In the process, they discover a way to handle their fears. The Christian faith offers a basis for honest and true relationships with other people, something most inmates have never had. There is hope for the future, a new sense of values, and an inner strength that comes through the Holy Spirit. The Christian who comes into a prison ministry comes with a precious and valuable message, and there are many eagerly waiting to receive it.

Perhaps above all, prisoners and those who minister to them need to see that God in Jesus Christ offers abundant life. Jesus said this was why He came (John 10:10). For the prisoner, this offer means new hope, a purpose for living, and love. That abundant life is for everyone—including prisoners.

CHAPTER 2 REVIEW QUESTIONS

1. The Bible has many examples, illustrations, and teachings concerning prisons, prisoners, and captivity of various kinds.
   a) True.
   b) False.

2. A Christian should visit those in prisons and jails because
   a) it is the right and humane thing to do.
   b) other Christians do it.
   c) Jesus commands Christians to make such visits.
   d) society expects this of church people.

3. Most prisoners are so caught up in their crimes and sins that there is no way for the gospel of Jesus Christ to have any meaning for them.
   a) True.
   b) False.

4. Despite harsh conditions in prisons, inmates not only accept the gospel but they are able to live their faith in prison and after release.
   a) True.
   b) False.

5. The Christian faith offers people in prisons
   a) forgiveness of sin.
   b) opportunity for repentance.
   c) acceptance of themselves.
   d) a sense of self-worth.
   e) hope.
   f) All of the above.

6. Being a faithful follower of Jesus will keep a person from being sent to jail or prison.
   a) True.
   b) False.

7. The Great Commission ("Go ye into all the world . . .") applies to typical church members as well as to missionaries.
   a) True.
   b) False.

8. Visiting those in prisons and jails is a Christian
   a) duty.
   b) obligation.
   c) responsibility.
   d) All of the above.

9. Church involvement with prison and jail visiting is a fairly recent development in the United States.
   a) True.
   b) False.

10. Inmates are so hardened by their way of life and by confinement that they are rarely interested in Jesus Christ.
    a) True.
    b) False.

3

Christian Volunteers in Penitentiaries and Prisons

You've heard the names on television or in films: San Quentin, Sing Sing, Alcatraz. Names like these bring images of fortress-like walls, guard towers, and row upon row of barred cells. Dark, ugly, depressing—yet they seem to have a perverse sort of glamor. Inmates call these places "the joint" or "inside." To most people they are penitentiaries and prisons. Whatever the term, these places are the temporary (and sometimes permanent) homes for hundreds of thousands of people, and new occupants move in every year.

In the federal prison system there are three levels of institutions. Maximum-security prisons are often referred to as penitentiaries. The medium-security facilities are often designated as federal correctional institutions, while the minimum-security units (often without walls) may be called camps or centers. The U.S. Bureau of Prisons operates almost fifty facilities around the nation: prisons, detention centers, camps, reception centers, and hospital prisons. The bureau also has contracts, usually with city or county jails, to hold federal prisoners awaiting sentencing.

Each state, of course, has its own prison system. These vary in size from Georgia, with seventy-six prisons, and Florida with forty-six, to six states that have only two prisons each.[1] A 1974 survey showed there were 400 state-operated prisons in the United States, plus almost 200 more confinement facilities of other types. About one-half of the state adult prisons are maximum-security units and about one-third are medium security. In 1977, these state institutions held an inmate population of almost 248,000.[2]

WHAT'S BEHIND THE BARS?

When you look through the prison walls, what do you see? Who are these people held apart from society and why are they there? There is always the danger of stereotyping inmates, just as there is with any group, but some generalities may help you understand the kind of people to whom the church is called to minister.

The 1970 census gave one of the clearest profiles of prisoners. They are generally young; one-third are under twenty-five and more than two-thirds are under thirty-five. More than half are white, although near the large metropolitan areas as many as three-quarters of new arrivals are black or Hispanic.[3] Almost half are single (many have never married). They are usually poorly educated (most haven't completed high school).

If you wonder where the women are, their relatively small number causes them to be almost invisible in the correctional system. Only about 3 percent of federal and state prisoners are women; that's about 8,000 in number. They are kept either in separate institutions or in separate parts of predominantly male prisons, but many of the problems and conditions that apply to men also apply to women offenders.

Various studies have tried to picture the typical offender. The President's Commission on Law Enforcement and Administration of Justice portrays the disadvantaged character of the offender. "The offender at the end of the road in prison is likely to be a member of the lowest social and economic group in the country, poorly educated and perhaps unemployed, unmarried, reared in a broken home, and to have a prior criminal record."[4]

Dr. Charles G. Wilson, director of research and planning for the Department of Corrections of North Carolina, has described the typical personality traits of the adult inmates he has studied. He sees an antisocial life-style, a resistance to efforts to control or modify personal behavior, and a rather limited sense of social responsibility. Inmates often have difficulty forming friendships or loyalties and are inclined to seek immediate satisfaction of their desires without considering the possible consequences. They tend to lack social judgment and have difficulty seeing what society expects of them in the way of socially acceptable behavior.[5]

Prisoners Are Individuals

When you go into a prison, however, you can't talk to the "typical" inmate; you can only talk to individuals, each a person with particular interests and feelings and experiences. I think of Bob, whom I met at a state prison in California. He is twenty-two years old, good-looking, and has a gentle spirit that the Lord is really using. Bob grew up in the streets, learned to fight and hold his own, and eventually became an amateur boxer. He married when he was seventeen, and he and his wife have two children. But he took a wrong turn and ended up in prison. He came one night to a Wednesday evening service at the prison chapel and later accepted Jesus Christ into his life.

The new Bob is a different person from the one who came into prison. He told me, "If I hadn't been arrested, I'd still have been lost. If God hadn't arrested me, I'd still not know Him." Bob is now at an honor camp with sixty other inmates, leading a Bible study and teaching others.

I think of Bob and Stu and Jackson and a host of other men, all individuals, each with needs and concerns, each to be cared for and related to, one by one. That's how Jesus ministered to people, and that's how you too must work if you are coming into a prison.

A Controlled Environment

Not only must you think of prisoners as individuals, but you must also accustom yourself to the environment of prisons if you are going to go into them. Indeed, the first rule of prison ministry is *learn and follow all the rules*.

You are immediately struck with the pervasive security and regimentation. That's a necessary part of prison life. You will need to know the visiting hours and who can come and who cannot. You will need to know what, if anything, can be brought in to a prisoner. You will have to learn where you can go and where you cannot. You will learn about "the count," the periodic physical counting of all inmates at times during the day. The count is a fact of prison life that must be recognized and never interfered with. You have to plan your ministry efforts around it.

Chaplain Frederick Silber, formerly with the Bureau of Prisons and now with corrections in the state of Ohio, emphasized this matter of the rules: "You must be aware of the structure and channels through which to go, the authority problems in an institution, the custody, the count, and all associated with these things as you minister among the staff and residents."[6] In short, recognize that you are coming into someone else's society; you are a guest in someone else's house and you must conform to his way of doing things.

The rules and procedures vary with the institution and with the level of security. This is why working through the chaplain is essential. He knows the rules and can show you how to minister most effectively and without interfering with prison routines.

Uneasy Feelings

When you first go into a prison as a volunteer you can expect to be overwhelmed, uneasy, and perhaps apprehensive, particularly if you are going into a medium- or maximum-security institution. Accept those feelings as natural; they happen in many unfamiliar situations. You may see conditions that are distressing to you, but you must look beyond the conditions at the people who are there. Each prison staff member, each correctional officer, each inmate is a human being, an individual, and you are there as a representative of Jesus Christ to show something of His love and concern for them. Focus on your reason for being there and soon you won't notice the surroundings.

The first time I was asked to speak at a major state prison, I went with a sense of high anticipation. I had been praying for God's direction for my ministry when, literally in the midst of that praying, the telephone rang and I was invited to come to this prison for a special worship occasion. When I went into the prison I did not see any prisoners; I saw only people I loved and who Christ loved. I saw only men to whom I could be a friend. I have stood outside the cells of men and talked with them through the bars, but the bars were not in the way. Jesus was there, reaching out to these men, and that was all that mattered.

THE VOLUNTEER: A KEY ROLE IN GOD'S PRISON TEAM

Many chaplains have told me that having good Christian volunteers means the difference between having an effective religious program in prisons and not having one. With hundreds or even thousands of inmates in a prison, the chaplain cannot provide the personal contact that is so important. Volunteers extend the chaplain's outreach and make him more effective. A report of the chaplaincy division of the Canadian Penitentiary Service showed that in most institutions the chaplain is unable to make meaningful contact with more than 20 to 25 percent of the inmate population. Through volunteers, however, that number can be doubled or even tripled.[7]

Volunteers are important to the inmate because the volunteer becomes another person to relate to from outside the prison system, a model of a balanced and mature life. The volunteer is someone to talk with and someone who will listen, perhaps even becoming a friend.

Volunteers are important to the families of inmates. They can provide encouragement and information and be of practical help as the family copes with their traumatic situation.

To the prison administrators, the volunteer represents an added resource for helping inmates with rehabilitation and eventual transition into society. The volunteer can provide services the institution itself cannot provide, at the same time helping to "humanize" the impersonal institutional processes.

The Christian volunteer is also important to his local church. He is a channel of communication, increasing awareness in the church and providing the other members with a focus for their prayers and support.

The committed volunteer is important to other volunteers. Prison volunteer work is often done in teams or small groups, and experienced volunteers can be encouragers, trainers, and examples to fellow believers, as well as witnesses to non-Christian volunteers.

Finally, the person who volunteers for ministry in prisons is important to himself. This ministry provides an avenue for the exercise of his abilities and an opportunity to put his faith into action. Sharing one's beliefs through a prison ministry can clarify and strengthen the faith of any believer.

What the Volunteer Can Do—on the Inside

But what exactly can a volunteer do in a prison religious program? More than you might realize. The specific tasks you may do are less important than the roles you fill. If you are working inside a prison, perhaps the most important thing you can do regarding inmates is simply to be there as an understanding friend and listener. Inmates don't need anyone else to tell them what to do or where they have gone wrong. They get enough of that. What they need is an understanding outsider, one who will listen and respond to them as individuals.

It can be a tremendous boost to an inmate if a volunteer-friend is available during crisis times. These may come, for example, when he faces a parole board or prior to release or when there is trouble in the family. Chaplains are often involved in crisis counseling. Having someone available for some in-depth caring can make a tremendous difference in how an inmate responds.

You can encourage new Christians. There are many of them in prisons and they need direction and help in Bible study, in devotions, and in all the disciplines that contribute to spiritual growth and maturity. You as a volunteer can provide that critical element of fellowship to men who so often feel alone in their faith.

As a Christian as well as a volunteer, you are a witness to your faith in Christ. Your consistent visits to the prison, your attitude of concern and caring for both staff and inmates, and your ability to share your faith in a low-key, nonaggressive manner will all be powerful evidences of the living faith you claim.

Finally, from inside the prison you can and should support the chaplain's program. He has a full range of activities that may need volunteer support, such as leading Bible studies, showing films, taking part in small sharing groups, or participating in prison worship services. Many chaplains can use administrative help: typing, telephoning, ordering literature. Your willingness to help will encourage the chaplain and help make his programs more effective in reaching the inmates.

What the Volunteer Can Do—on the Outside

There is also much you can do as a Christian volunteer from outside the prison. Prayer is the first and fundamental ministry—prayer for the chaplains, prayer for particular inmates, and prayer for other volunteers.

Another significant ministry that can be done from your own home is writing to prisoners. Mail is eagerly anticipated in prison life. One inmate called it "paper sunshine." Some organizations (such as, Visit By Mail, % Christian Prison Volunteers, Box 1949, Hollywood, CA 90028) can provide the names of inmates who want correspondents or you can write to most prison chaplains. Our office maintains a list of many hundreds of prisoners from all around the nation who would like to have pen pals. New names come in every week. Their letters plead for someone to write to, someone who will be a friend, someone who will care. Positive, encouraging letters, picture postcards, photographs, and birthday and holiday cards can make the difference between a prisoner regaining his confidence and self-respect or remaining angry and isolated from society—and from Christ.

Another ministry that can be done from the outside is caring for the families of prisoners. This is an outreach that is particularly suitable for a husband-wife team or for ladies from your church. (To prevent misunderstandings it is important that men do not visit the family alone.) These families need material support, emotional encouragement, and spiritual nurture at a time when they are wrestling with social stigma, isolation, and very often a feeling of being overwhelmed by events beyond their control.

Beyond these ministries, there is the important work of helping released inmates readjust to society. There are many needs, such as serving as a parole or probation sponsor or finding employment, for which inmates will require counsel and guidance and for which volunteers can play a vital role.

Inside or outside prison walls, Christian volunteers have many opportunities to express their faith and compassion in visible ways toward the men and women in America's penal institutions. Behind the forbidding prison walls are people Jesus can love through you and me. Will we let Him?

CHAPTER 3 REVIEW QUESTIONS

1. The number of state and federal prisons is
   a) about 1,200.
   b) about 400 to 500.
   c) less than 100.

2. The levels of security which exist in the federal prison system are
   a) maximum and minimum.
   b) maximum, minimum, and detention.
   c) minimum, medium, and maximum.
   d) maximum, medium, and detention.

3. The typical person in a prison can be described as
   a) an habitual criminal.
   b) young, white, single, and poorly educated.
   c) young, black, and male.

4. About one-fourth of all persons in prison are women.
   a) True.
   b) False.

5. When working with prisoners, it is good to keep in mind the characteristics of the typical inmate. Then you will know what to expect when talking with an individual inmate.
   a) True.
   b) False.

6. The first and fundamental rule of ministering in prisons is
   a) to take nothing in or out.
   b) to follow all the rules.
   c) to know the visiting hours.

7. When you first go into a prison as a volunteer, you can expect to be overwhelmed, uneasy, and apprehensive.
   a) True.
   b) False.

8. Christian volunteers can be an important part of a prison's religious program.
   a) True.
   b) False.

9. Sharing your faith with an inmate should be done in
   a) a low-key, nonaggressive manner.
   b) a forceful, direct way.
   c) response to questions from the inmate only.

10. The only way to really minister to prison inmates is by going inside the prison for face-to-face meetings.
    a) True.
    b) False.

4

Christian Volunteers in Local Jails

Of America's various correctional institutions, it is the thousands of jails that confine the most people with the greatest needs but for whom the least is being done. Yet I believe jails have the largest potential for Christian ministrv within the entire correctional system.

Jails are very different from prisons. Both confine people and both may be crowded, but beyond that there are numerous differences. Prison inmates have been tried and convicted of crimes. Jail inmates often have not been convicted of anything; many are being held pending trial. The prison population is comparatively stable, as inmates tend to serve longer sentences. A jail population is highly transient; new offenders are brought in while others are released or transferred to other institutions. Inmates in any one prison are all under one jurisdiction—either state or federal. A jail, on the other hand, may simultaneously hold persons accused of offenses under federal, state, county, or city laws. Prisons have at least a minimum of facilities and programs for counseling and rehabilitation. Most jails have few or none.

A jail is defined as "a locally operated facility authorized to retain persons for forty-eight hours or longer." That longer period typically extends up to twelve months. A jail is intended to be a pretrial detention center, a place to hold people until their cases are heard in court, but they have become more than just detention centers. They are also being used as short-term correctional institutions for people charged with less serious crimes and as way stations for an assortment of other defendants who will eventually move on to other institutions.

Jails range from small one- or two-cell units in the back of a police station or courthouse to the multi-story buildings found in our larger cities which house thousands of inmates. Cook County Jail in Chicago has 4,000 to 5,000 inmates at any given time. A 1972 survey showed that the average jail in Washington, D.C., held about 700 inmates, those in New York held an average of 200, and those in California, Massachusetts, and New Jersey held more than 100 each.[1]

Jails are usually at the end of the line in most city and county budgets, so most are limited in the facilities and programs that can be provided beyond bare necessities. A 1970 survey of the nation's jails revealed that 89 percent had no educational facilities or programs for inmates, 86 percent had no recreational facilities, about 50 percent had no medical facilities, and about 25 percent had no visiting rooms.[2] More harsh words have probably been written about jails than about any other penal institution, but this negative view reflects, in part, the lack of interest and awareness by local citizens concerning the needs of jails. As one news magazine reported concerning why jail conditions are so poor, "Most authorities agree it is because the general public does not know what goes on inside them and often couldn't care less."[3] If more people took an active interest in their local jails, the conditions might improve.

THE UNIQUE NEEDS OF JAIL INMATES

What this means to those engaged in jail ministries is that the physical, emotional, and psychological conditions are different from and less favorable than those in prisons. There is usually no privacy in which to meet or talk with individual inmates. More often than not, the volunteer is standing outside a holding cage or cell, talking through bars to one or more people inside—assuming they want to listen. The prisoners are often bored, restless, and fearful. Ed Stelle, police chaplain for the Portland, Oregon city-county jails, told me, "Prisoners live in the cells twenty-four hours a day, but the worst of it is they are all there *waiting*. They don't know when they are going to trial, when they are going to court; they don't know the outcome of the trial. Uncertainty is their life."

Enforced boredom is the rule, so prisoners may show an interest in a volunteer's approach or in a religious program simply because there is nothing else to do. The volunteer may also be seen as a possible help in getting out of jail, and inmates may seek favors from the volunteer.

Prisoners are often exposed to potential violence, and this fear strongly affects many inmates. Urban jails, particularly, are plagued by high rates of attempted and completed suicide. Many times these suicides are committed by drug addicts who think death is their only relief from the horror and anxiety of withdrawal symptoms.

Illumination in the cells may be poor, making it difficult for prisoners to read literature the volunteer may hand out. There is noise all the time: steel doors banging, radios or televisions blaring, announcements on a public-address system, people shouting and moving about continuously. This simply means jail conditions will be far from ideal for effective communication. A jail volunteer worker must be flexible and able to adjust to difficult conditions.

But did Jesus call you to an easy ministry when He said, "Follow Me"?

Differences between Jail and Prison Inmates

Jail inmates resemble prison inmates in some respects, but there are differences too. The jail population is not only transient but highly mixed. Alcoholics, drug addicts, prostitutes, and troubled youngsters all end up in jails—sometimes in the same cells. Professor Edith Flynn has described jail as "the traditional dumping ground for the untried, the petty offender, the vagrant, the debtor and beggar, the promiscuous, and the mentally ill."[4]

The 1972 LEAA survey revealed a profile of jail inmates: 95 percent are male; 9 percent are juveniles (under eighteen); 42 percent are black; half have never married; two-thirds have not completed high school.[5] In addition, those in jail are frequently poor; indeed, many remain in jail because they cannot afford the bail.

THE EFFECTIVE JAIL MINISTRY

Can anything be done? Yes, many things, but the key and absolutely essential ingredient to effective jail ministry is the support of the jail administrators—the sheriff, chief of police, head jailer, or whoever is responsible in your particular community. Ideally, you want not only their agreement to a religious program but their backing. The jail staff is often overworked and underpaid, and they may see volunteers as an intrusion and a nuisance. They will need to be convinced that volunteers will help them in some way, or at least not unduly interfere with their responsibilities.

You must develop the trust and confidence of the jail staff. Chaplain Stelle said, "You must stay within the framework of the privilege you have been given to work in that jail. Once the jailers understand what you're doing and get to trust you, they'll support you. With prayer, this kind of rapport can be established. But once you lose the trust and confidence of the jailers, you can't get it back."

Despite the distracting environment and the less-than-welcome attitude by some jailers and inmates, I am convinced that effective jail ministries are possible and that these ministries can and must be based on the work of local churches and individual Christians. Perhaps the most practical form of ministry (and sometimes the only one possible) is consistent visitation.

Simply *being there* as one who cares and is willing to listen is an exceedingly valuable ministry. As Chaplain Stelle pointed out, "Jail inmates are people without much hope, and the only people who are coming in there with any semblance of hope are sometimes their attorney, or occasionally a family member, and in some places those with the message of Christ."

Distributing literature and Bibles may be possible, when approved by the jail administration. The American Bible Society has an extensive program of supplying Bibles to correctional institutions (although most of these are prisons and there is still a need in many jails). In some jails, Bible correspondence courses may be distributed and sent. Chaplain Phil Wagner at Cook County Jail has an extensive correspondence course ministry using the Emmaus materials. A weekly worship service is perhaps the most common ministry in many jails. Sometimes there are more than one a week if different denominations are involved. Bible study classes and discussion groups may also be possible, particularly in the larger jails, and interest among inmates can be high. Other programs may include film showings, traveling evangelists, musical groups, and personal or small-group counseling.

A jail ministry in Portland, Oregon, headed by a police chaplain, trains selected local pastors as team leaders. Each team consists of other pastors, church lay people, or Bible school students—all trained to meet the needs of jail inmates. At the large Cook County Jail in Chicago, volunteers under the guidance of chaplains and experienced volunteers conduct Bible study classes, offer and grade Bible correspondence courses, assist with worship services, and encourage Christian inmates who in turn may lead Bible studies in the cell blocks.

Organizations with merely humanitarian motives can sometimes provide ways for Christians to become involved with jails and prisons. One agency I know recruits and trains volunteers to work one-to-one with young adult prisoners in jails awaiting trial. Volunteers are given several weeks of training, including a visit to a prison or jail, lectures, role-playing, and films. Volunteers commit themselves to a particular inmate for at least a year and spend one evening a week with him. This commitment continues whether the prisoner is released, transferred to a state prison, or stays in jail. Agencies of this sort represent another channel through which individual Christians can become familiar with jail-oriented programs.

While many jails are similar, there are differences in the potential for volunteer work in general and for religious ministry in particular. Some facilities will allow for a greater variety of activities than others. A change of jail administrators may bring a new openness to volunteers. On the other hand, it may inhibit efforts and require time and new resolve to continue in spite of setbacks. You will need to be alert to every possibility and seek ways to expand the outreach to jail inmates.

VOLUNTEER MINISTRY AT OTHER INSTITUTIONS

Often overlooked are the other kinds of correctional institutions—juvenile detention halls, reformatories, work release centers, correctional camps, and work farms. These institutions may be almost invisible in a community and hence neglected as places of potential ministry. The level of security in these facilities varies from minimum to very secure, but where there is less security there is often greater potential for volunteers and for a greater variety of programs. While some of these institutions, especially for juveniles, may have a full-time or part-time chaplain, most have neither chaplains nor any type of organized, consistent religious program of Christian witness. There is great potential here for both churches and for individual Christians.

Juveniles

Work with juveniles is an important type of correctional rehabilitative work because of the potential for keeping young people out of prisons altogether (diversion) or helping them to avoid following a manner of life that will bring them back into prison. Juveniles may be offenders or ex-offenders, those charged with minor crimes or those involved in serious offenses, children who have been abandoned or neglected, emotionally disturbed youth, and those from broken and disrupted homes.

Juveniles in confinement are numerous in quantity as well as diverse in their needs. The National Council on Crime and Delinquency estimated in 1966 that 100,000 children aged seven to seventeen were detained in county jails and police lockups each year, and another 400,000 were held in detention institutions at some time during the year.[6] Half a million young people in confinement—and there's no indication that those figures have significantly decreased in recent years. Unfortunately, most jails provide no programs of recreation or education for juveniles, and in many cases juveniles are placed with adult offenders.

Most detention homes for juveniles cannot refuse children assigned to them; they must take every child referred by the police or the courts and hold him until the court orders his release. Tragically, some children spend years in detention homes.

Church groups should approach detention centers in the same manner as a jail. Talk to the person in charge. Find out some of the needs of the center. Point out what you and your group can provide and do. Typical programs could include small Bible study and discussion groups oriented to the needs and interests of young people; classes in arts, crafts, music, or personal grooming; distribution of literature, recordings, or craft supplies; arranging for birthday parties or gifts; and even taking group outings. The possibilities are limited only by the requirements of the institution or your own imagination and enthusiasm.

There are three primary areas of juvenile programs where volunteers are helpful: diversion programs, offenders in confinement, and as counselors or sponsors for those released on parole or probation.

For example, in California the M-2 program, a nonprofit organization under contract to the California Department of Corrections, matches offenders with volunteers who offer regular visitation, one-to-one counseling, and placement in jobs or full-time schooling. The program has seen positive results, and offenders involved in this program were more successful on parole than those who were not involved.

During a nine-year period, a Volunteer Counselor Program in Lincoln, Nebraska has seen 350 citizens volunteer their time to work with more than 500 young people aged sixteen to twenty who were charged with minor crimes and are now released on probation. Offenders and volunteers are carefully selected and matched to insure a compatible relationship. Volunteers are recruited from community groups, churches, and personal contacts. One-fourth of those who apply are turned down, but those who are accepted are given a ten-hour training course in counseling and crisis intervention skills, plus a psychological test to help with the matching process. Volunteers spend about ten months with the young people they are assigned to, meeting with them in the evenings or on weekends.

While programs such as these are not specifically church related, they illustrate the kinds of programs through which a Christian might work, as well as the kinds of training and preparation that are needed to be effective. With juvenile programs the hope is that the volunteer's impact will be an important element in keeping the young person from future imprisonment. That is a hope worthy of any Christian's best effort.

The challenge of jails, detention centers, work farms, and similar institutions is that they are among the most overlooked in terms of volunteer programs. Because these institutions are often in the area of a local church or a group of concerned Christians, they represent an excellent potential for outreach. Literally millions of men, women, and children pass through America's jails every year, and most of them will find nothing in that unpleasant experience to remind them of God or to point them to a new life. They will find nothing, that is, unless Christians become involved. Jesus is in jail, too, and He waits for your visit. When will you come?

CHAPTER 4 REVIEW QUESTIONS

1. Since there are many more jails than prisons, it is reasonable to assume that more is being done for spiritual minis tries in jails than in prisons.
   a) True.
   b) False.

2. A jail can detain a person for as long as one year.
   a) True.
   b) False.

3. The conditions most likely to exist in a typical jail are
   a) individual cells for each prisoner.
   b) large cells that hold several or many prisoners.
   c) extensive cell-blocks, like many prisons.

4. Talking effectively with a jail inmate in his cell may be difficult because of
   a) noise from other inmates, radios, banging of doors, etc.
   b) lack of privacy.
   c) indifference of inmates.
   d) All of the above.

5. In jail ministry, the most important aspect is
   a) gaining the trust and confidence of the chief jailer and guards.
   b) being thoroughly grounded in the Bible.
   c) having enough volunteers to keep the program going.

6. Many people stay in jail awaiting trial because
   a) they know they're guilty so they don't try to leave.
   b) they are too poor to afford bail.
   c) they don't know how to contact a lawyer.

7 Christian ministries that can be done in many jails are
a) worship services, personal witnessing, literature distribution, Bible studies, and others.
b) only worship services.
c) only worship services and film showings.

8. Since juvenile offenders are treated differently and detained separately from adult offenders, there are few or no opportunities for ministry to juveniles in jail.
a) True.
b) False.

9. During a typical year, the approximate number of juveniles held in various detention facilities is
a) less than 100,000.
b) 400,000 or more.
c) one million or more.

10. Church members can often serve as counselors and as sponsors to young people on probation.
a) True.
b) False.

5

The Prison Chaplain and the Volunteer: A Ministry Team

Over the years I have met many prison and jail chaplains. They have come from different church backgrounds—Baptist, Methodist, Presbyterian, and many others—but in every case I have been tremendously impressed with their dedication and commitment to the correctional ministry. The men and women who serve as chaplains in jails, prisons, detention halls, and similar places of confinement are truly Christ's ambassadors behind bars. The Bible tells us to honor those who preach and teach God's Word, and prison chaplains are certainly worthy of this honor.

Chaplains work long hours under difficult conditions, dealing with personal crises of inmates every day, providing programs that try to meet the spiritual needs of inmates, and fighting the frustrations and disappointments that are an integral part of the prison chaplaincy. In addition most have family responsibilities of their own.

Full-time prison and jail chaplains may have more training and preparation for their work than do some ministers. Before a potential chaplain can be accepted into most federal or state prisons, he or she usually must have completed seminary training and be endorsed by a denomination or church body. Many chaplains have served in pastorates before coming to the chaplaincy; they may have completed an internship in an institutional chaplaincy; and they may have had special graduate training in counseling. The chaplain must also be acceptable to the warden of the prison in which he is to work.

With this preparation, a chaplain functions as the administrator of a religious program for the entire institution. Basically, he must provide for the traditional preaching and worship functions, oversee a religious education program, and spend much of his time in personal counseling. In addition, he must allow time for administrative activities (writing letters, attending meetings, preparing reports), recruiting and supervising volunteers, assisting inmates' families, and speaking at local churches. Somewhere in the midst of all this he must attend to his personal spiritual life. In short, the typical prison chaplain is a very busy person!

A survey taken by the Bureau of Prisons asked inmates and prison staff what they thought the role of the prison chaplain should be. The overwhelming view of the chaplain was that of a worship leader; he must take the lead in providing opportunities for inmates to worship. The role of counselor follows closely. Inmates seek out the chaplain for many reasons. They may have personal problems, either within the prison or at home. Others see the chaplain as an approachable member of the institution staff, someone with whom they can talk. Still others have genuine spiritual concerns and are seeking help to grow in faith.

The chaplain, too, must be aware of the institutions's requirements. His programs and activities must not interfere with the rules and procedures of the prison or jail, yet he must do all he can to be available to the inmates. Some chaplains consider the prison staff a part of their concern, while others focus almost exclusively on the prisoners. A balance is necessary.

In light of all the demands upon chaplains, most want and can use volunteers in their religious programs. One study of prison chaplains found that the average Protestant chaplain (mainly in prisons) had about twenty-five volunteers, while the average Catholic chaplain had about a dozen.[1] The chaplain is responsible for recruiting and screening potential volunteers, as well as for providing them with some training and supervision. How much and how well this is done varies with the individual chaplain. Some coordinate programs that volunteers conduct, while others use volunteers within programs they have already started. In either case, a good relationship between chaplain and volunteer is critical to an effective ministry in the prison or jail.

THE CHAPLAIN/VOLUNTEER RELATIONSHIP

The key to that relationship is for the chaplain to lead and the volunteer to follow. The chaplain is responsible for the presence and activities of volunteers in the prison, and if something goes wrong he will bear the brunt of the criticism. All potential volunteers must approach the institutional chaplain (if there is one) in order to begin a ministry there. The chaplain is the person to turn to first for all problems and questions concerning the prison system or the relationship with the inmates. In some situations volunteers have bypassed the chaplain, either to the prison administration or to the inmate, and the result has always been embarrassment, bad feelings, and a loss of stature for the religious ministry.

Any person who expects to work as a volunteer within a prison or jail must be willing to follow, support, and take direction from the chaplain. Not every volunteer is willing to do that, chaplains have told me. If a person is unwilling to take direction from the person responsible for the program, I would have to suggest that he seek to minister elsewhere.

Any volunteer working within an established prison or jail religious program should always support that program rather than criticize it to the inmates. When a volunteer has differences of opinion or suggestions for improvements concerning some aspect of the religious program, it is only considerate and proper to discuss those views with the chaplain. It is not a good testimony of Christian unity or charity for Christians to speak badly about the efforts of other Christians.

One of the chaplain's responsibilities toward volunteers is that of orienting and training new volunteers. That orientation should basically cover the institution, the religious program, and the inmates. Many chaplains arrange for various prison officials to describe the prison system, how it works, and what its rules and procedures are. This knowledge is basic to a prison ministry; any volunteer must have a general understanding of how the institution functions.

But as one chaplain said, "Since the administration tends to focus on the negatives—the do's and don'ts—I try to focus on the positives and what can be done." An orientation to the prison's religious program should also describe its objectives, its various activities, and how volunteers can contribute to the program. Finally, the chaplain should describe the inmates, who they are generally, and how to work with them effectively. Some chaplains may be able to discuss principles of counseling and techniques for small-group leadership.

It is important that volunteers not hesitate to ask questions, either during orientation or at any later time. You can never learn everything at one exposure, and you will encounter situations you will have questions about. Consider your volunteering an experience of continual learning, where each visit to a prison and each contact with an inmate will suggest new questions and bring new insights.

Without the chaplain, the volunteer can do little or nothing. Without the volunteer, the chaplain will always be limited in the extent of his outreach and the depth of his impact. Together, the committed chaplain and the trained volunteer can become a ministry team that brings Christian caring and compassion to many thousands of prisoners who might otherwise never find any hope or redemption.

The Prison Chaplain and the Volunteer: A Ministry Team

CHAPTER 5 REVIEW QUESTIONS

1. Most prison chaplains have had special training for chaplaincy work in addition to standard pastoral education.
   a) True.
   b) False.

2. The most frequent duties of a chaplain are
   a) administrator, counselor, and worship leader.
   b) pastor, volunteer coordinator, and religious education director.
   c) administrator and preacher.

3. Most chaplains want and can use volunteers in prison religious programs.
   a) True.
   b) False.

4. The best way to describe a good working relationship between volunteer and chaplain is
   a) pastor—church member.
   b) leader—follower.
   c) teacher—student.

5. If a volunteer in the religious program does not like something about the prison or its religious program, he should first
   a) write or speak directly to the warden or senior official.
   b) complain to the guards.
   c) discuss it with the chaplain.
   d) write a letter to the editor of the local paper.

6. Since the chaplain may be very busy, the best way for a volunteer to learn more about a prison is by
   a) observing carefully.
   b) asking questions.
   c) reading more books.

7. If a volunteer wants to bring literature into the prison for the inmates, he should get permission from
   a) a guard.
   b) the chaplain.
   c) the volunteer coordinator.

8. In a prison ministry, the key relationship is between
   a) volunteers.
   b) volunteer and the chaplain.
   c) volunteer and the volunteer coordinator.

9. If something goes wrong in a prison religious volunteer program, the responsibility is placed upon the
   a) volunteer.
   b) coordinator of volunteers.
   c) chaplain.
   d) prison or jail administrator.

10. A prison volunteer can expect to learn about the prison and its programs from
    a) the chaplain's instruction.
    b) films and publications.
    c) tours of facilities.
    d) All of the above.

6

The Inmate and the Volunteer: A Caring Relationship

"I loved my mother and showed her how much I loved her by coming to this hell hole. Now she has to take the trouble to come down here and visit me. She's the only friend I've got now."[1]

Thirty-four-year-old James is serving a thirty-year sentence at New Jersey's Rahway State Prison. His comment reflects some of the self-hate and anguish felt by so many inmates and is typical of the kinds of feelings any volunteer worker may encounter in prisons and jails. Like James, many prisoners have no one who really cares what happens to them, unless it's a mother or some other family member—or a Christian volunteer.

Most prisoners have experienced a life that has been full of disappointment, failure, fear, resentment, guilt, and nothing to give them hope for anything better. What do you say to such people about a God of love and caring, or of a Savior who offers new life? What can a prisoner see in you to make him believe you are different from all the other people he has ever known?

When you go into a prison or jail, you will meet all kinds of people in many different situations. You will meet the person with prior prison terms and the first-time offender. Some are sorry for their past and others seem to have no awareness of or concern for their wrongdoing. Some will be Christians, some will follow non-Christian beliefs, and others will have no apparent interest in their spiritual condition. Each will be an individual, but you must be open to ministering to all.

YOUR FIRST DAY IN PRISON

When you first begin work in a prison or a large jail, the chaplain will probably be the one to bring you in touch with the inmates. He may introduce you to one specific individual with whom you might develop a one-to-one relationship, or you may meet a group of inmates, perhaps in a Bible study or in a worship service. From the very start, you will need to let them know you are there out of genuine concern and compassion for them as persons, and because you believe this is what your Lord would have you to do.

Naturally, at first they won't believe your statements to that effect. You will be checked out, tested, and given a hard look to see if you are the person you claim to be. Most inmates have been "used" so much in their lives that they think it is natural, so you can expect some of them to try to "use" you. They may ask you to do small favors, and then make you feel cheap or petty if you refuse. They will test you to see how much annoyance and rebuff you can take. Paradoxically, if you do the favor or lose your patience, you also lose their respect.

Your hope should be to develop a relationship with one or a few inmates to the point where they will trust you and recognize that you are genuinely interested in them as persons. This relationship and rapport will come as a result of your consistent visitation, your understanding and listening, and the development of mutual interests. You want to nurture and encourage the human spirit in all the people you meet, and to fan whatever spark of goodness or hope that exists in that person.

Remember that inmates often have a very poor self-image and they will expect you to treat them as so many others have done.

Becoming a prisoner is a traumatic experience. The offender is stripped of his normal identity and relationships, loses freedom of choice and action, lacks privacy, is totally dependent upon strangers (prison and jail staff), and must conform to unusual schedules for all the routines of life, such as eating, sleeping, and bathing. "It means becoming someone else, someone less, in a new and unfamiliar place."[2] As a volunteer, you must reckon with the experience and trauma of most inmates and seek to help the inmate build up a positive view of himself, as a person of worth and of potential. That is how God sees that inmate; can you see it too?

Learn the Prison "Lingo"

You will need to be attuned to the language of prison, yet be able to speak with inmates in a clear, simple way without a lot of "church talk." Big words like "justification" or "salvation" don't carry much meaning for most inmates; they may even convey some wrong impressions. John Wesley, the noted English preacher, spoke about all the important Bible doctrines to thousands of people, but he always made a great effort to be understood by the person of even the least education. "I design plain truth for plain people," he once said. "I labour to avoid all words which are not easy to understand, all which are not used in common life." Make that your aim too, when talking with an inmate, teaching a class, or leading a group discussion. You are not there to show off your learning and knowledge, but to stand aside and let others see Jesus.

Be Sensitive During Crisis Periods

As a volunteer, you need to be aware that there are certain times in the life of an offender when he feels strong pressures and anxieties. It is at times like these that you can be especially welcome as a friend and understanding listener. Four "crisis periods" are particularly important: following arrest, just prior to and after a trial, during the first few weeks in prison, and just prior to release. This is not to say there are not other times when an offender is feeling a crisis, but these four periods are often mentioned by chaplains.

Just after a person has been arrested he is isolated from friends and family and feels great anxiety and uncertainty about what will happen to him. It may be several days before he can get in touch with anyone on the outside to let them know where he is. A person in jail may be there many weeks before his trial, wondering what will happen while the suspense and worry build. By the time of his trial, the accused person is under tremendous pressure. Following a trial, he may return to jail awaiting appeal or transfer to another institution. It is another time of great uncertainty.

The first few weeks in prison are also times of stress and uncertainty, especially if this is the person's first prison sentence, as he learns his way around and tries to decide which group of inmates he will associate with. His decisions during this early period can influence the rest of his prison stay, and if he decides to be part of those inmates who are Christians or who at least are active in prison religious activities, the newcomer will probably continue with that group throughout his confinement.

The weeks and even months prior to release from prison are also stressful. The inmate has become accustomed to a highly structured society where he has little decision-making to do. Now he is about to be thrust out into a far less structured society where he will have to make many decisions and where he will have to rebuild broken or strained personal relationships. This means that release, while it is greatly desired, is also looked on with anxiety and even fearfulness. One of the most helpful things volunteers can do at release time is to be sure there is someone waiting to meet him when he walks out of the prison door. A warm greeting can do much at this critical time.

In addition to these periods of stress, inmates may experience personal crises at any time. A letter from the family may tell of illness or financial struggles. A loved one may die. Other inmates may bring pressure for various reasons. Chaplains spend much of their time dealing with these crises, but a volunteer who has developed a good relationship with an inmate may also be a valuable counselor and source of strength and encouragement at such times.

Don't Forget Female Prisoners

There is a special need for Christian women who will volunteer to work with female inmates. Women in prisons and jails are often isolated from the mainstream of institutional life and are left with nothing to do and no real opportunity for rehabilitation. What is often overlooked is that female inmates may be mothers and even wage earners for their families. One estimate said that on any given day there are 21,000 children of imprisoned mothers. When the mother is arrested, the children may be removed from their home and school and not allowed to see their parent. Both mother and children suffer anxiety because of this unnatural separation. Christian women volunteers who counsel, befriend, and act as models for these women inmates provide a desperately needed ministry that is often neglected.

SHARING YOUR FAITH WITH INMATES

Sharing one's faith is a concern of the Christian prison volunteer, but that faith must come through in more than words. I mentioned earlier the importance of personal example as a strong witness to inmates. They will look at what you are and what you do before they will listen to what you say. But at some point there will come an opportunity to respond to an inmate's interest in why you are a volunteer or what your faith consists of. By that time you should have an idea of where the inmate is in his awareness and understanding of the Christian faith and how he sees his own spiritual condition. Unless you know where he is, you won't know where to start.

Your personal testimony may be appropriate if you can phrase it in nonreligious language. Help the inmate to see that from God's point of view, the separation of all mankind from Himself is the primary issue to be resolved, not the breaking of some man-made laws. Paul, in his letter to the church at Ephesus, calls on the Ephesian Christians to remember what they once were: separated from Christ, foreigners, having no part in the covenants with God, without hope and without God. He also reminded them that they had been spiritually dead, following the evil ways of this world and living accordingly to their bodily desires.

That's where you were at one time, as well as that man or woman you are talking with on the other side of the bars. You have no righteousness of your own to boast of; you have been saved through the grace of God in Jesus Christ—so don't let the inmate think you are somehow inherently "better" than he is. He is doubly imprisoned: physically, because of man's laws, and spiritually, because of the sin that separates him from God. You can hold out the great hope, as Paul wrote to the Galatians, that "Freedom is what we have—Christ has set us free! . . ." (Gal. 5:1, TEV).

Along with your personal testimony you may get an opportunity to share something from the Bible. If the inmate does not have his own Bible, ask the chaplain how one may be obtained. If you can encourage an inmate to begin to read the Bible, perhaps along with some appropriate Christian literature or a Bible correspondence course, you will not only be encouraging his Christian growth but you will be providing a positive use of his time and a witness by example to other inmates.

With inmates who are already Christians, you will want to focus on building them up in the faith. One comment chaplains have made repeatedly is the need for in-depth Christian training. As one chaplain told me, "Many inmates have had many startings of religious experience—baptism, raising of hands, going forward—but so many have never gone ahead in depth in their Christian life." You will encounter new Christians who will need all the encouragement and training you can give, and sometimes you will even meet Christian inmates who can teach *you* something about the Christian life. I remember Bob, at San Quentin, a Christian inmate who had an active ministry among his fellow prisoners. He told me one time, "Where else should I be? God put me here. These are the only people I know in the world, and

I'm here to be a witness and a testimony to them." Bob knew he was truly free despite his surroundings. "There are thirty-foot walls all around and bars on my windows—but I'm free!"

You can continue to encourage a Christian inmate through correspondence, sending helpful literature, and when he is released, by helping him get established in a church. You may also have the opportunity to share with the inmate's family and help them understand the new life that has come to this one who was in prison.

IT'S NOT AN EASY ROAD

I don't want to give you the idea that building a relationship with an inmate is a smooth process from initial introduction to coming to a knowledge of Christ. This is not the case with persons outside prisons and it certainly is not true for those in prisons. Some inmates are not interested in spiritual matters. They are willing to talk about other things but will "turn off" when religious matters arise. Some will completely reject you, curse you, and want to have nothing to do with you.

Others will try to use the relationship with you to further their own ends. Inmates tend to look for what they can get immediately and they often see other people as objects to be used, much as they themselves have been used. Their attitude may be, "What can you do for me today?" Even God and religion are considered things to be manipulated. Many chaplains can tell of "thirty-day conversion"—inmates try to use the language of faith and prayer, then reject God and the Bible because they get no "results."

On the other hand, there are prisoners who truly repent and are converted. Chaplain Austin Brown of the state prison in Starke, Florida comments; "We know these men and we can usually tell if they're sincere or not. Some of these men are being saved, and that's the first step toward rehabilitation."[3] From the state prison at Alto, Georgia, Chaplain Steve Doran says, "The main way you can tell is to watch the prisoner over a period of time. Lots of times a man's behavior pattern changes and his disciplinary reports stop."[4]

It may help to recall Jesus' parable of the sower of seed and the four kinds of soil upon which the seed fell. Inmates, like everyone else, will fit into one of these four types of responsiveness to the gospel. As a volunteer, you must be sensitive to this problem of false profession without becoming cynical about every profession of faith. Sometimes you will have to move on, seeking more receptive inmates. Other times you may need to patiently "water the ground" and let God's Spirit bring about a change in "soil quality" in the heart and mind of an inmate. You will need prayer, faithfulness, and spiritual discernment for this work—a high standard, but our service for Jesus demands nothing less.

Another disappointment for some volunteers may be the lack of continuing contact with an inmate after he is released or is transferred. You may have developed an open, trusting relationship with an inmate only to discover that soon he will no longer be there. In some cases you may be able to stay in touch by mail, but don't be surprised if you hear nothing further from your friend. Particularly those who have been released may want to have nothing to do with anyone who reminds them of their prison experience, even if that person was helpful to them. Prison was a painful time and they would like to shut out all memories.

What is sometimes possible (and perhaps in some ways preferable) is to put the ex-inmate in contact with some Christian person in his community and encourage a new friendship to be established. This provides a break with the past while at the same time providing continuing Christian fellowship and nurture to this person who is adjusting to the outside world. Every situation is different, however, and you must treat each person individually.

As each person with whom you have worked is released back to family, friends, and society, say a prayer of thanksgiving that God allowed you the opportunity to come into that person's life and reflect something of Jesus Christ to him. You will feel regret at not doing more or not saying the right things, but ask God to give you His wisdom for the next inmate you will meet.

CHAPTER 6 REVIEW QUESTIONS

1. All inmates have about the same attitude toward their crimes.
   a) True.
   b) False.

2. Your aim in developing relationships with inmates should be
   a) for them to respect you as a teacher.
   b) for them to trust you and see your interest in them as persons.
   c) for them to treat you as a "buddy."

3. There are certain times of particular stress or crisis for most inmates. These include
   a) following arrest, prior to and after a trial, upon entering prison, and prior to release.
   b) awaiting trial, halfway through the prison sentence, just prior to release, and just after release.
   c) following arrest, when there is a family crisis, and upon entering prison.

4. Women volunteers can be effective in prison ministries, especially with other women and with juveniles.
   a) True.
   b) False.

5. The most important part of a Christian's witness to prisoners is
   a) thorough knowledge of the Bible.
   b) ability to speak easily with others.
   c) a personal life consistent with biblical teaching.

6. For inmates who are Christians, the volunteer's concern should be
   a) fellowship.
   b) encouraging a witness to fellow prisoners.
   c) teaching and training for depth in spiritual life.
   d) All of the above.

7. Some attitudes Christian volunteers can expect among prisoners are
   a) indifference.
   b) rejection.
   c) welcome.
   d) manipulation.
   e) All of the above.
   f) Only a) and d).

8. After a person is released from prison, he may very well
   a) break off all further contact with the volunteer.
   b) seek out the volunteer for help.
   c) keep up correspondence by mail.

9. Since some inmates will make false professions of faith to gain favor, there is no point in seeking conversions among prisoners.
   a) True.
   b) False.

10. Even when a prisoner makes a sincere profession, there is no way for him to demonstrate his changed life.
   a) True.
   b) False.

7

How to Be an Effective Volunteer

A good volunteer must be dependable.
A volunteer must follow the rules.
Volunteers must be good listeners.

Everyone seems to have his own view on what makes a good volunteer in prison and jail ministries, so I decided to ask a group of chaplains what they thought an effective Christian volunteer should be like.

Consistency and dependability seem to be everyone's concern. Phil Wagner, Protestant chaplain at Chicago's huge Cook County Jail, says, "Our problem is that a lot of volunteers don't stay. They come in on an 'ego trip,' thinking this is an exciting ministry. But after five or six weeks it gets tedious coming week after week, or they find they're dealing with a difficult group or facing a lot of hard questions, and they just drop out and we never see them again. A good volunteer is someone who will come down *every* week, who will memorize the names of the people he is caring for, and who will be praying for those people during the week."

Phil's comments are echoed by Manford Craig, Protestant chaplain at the large federal penitentiary at Leavenworth: "I get a lot of well-meaning people who say, 'I'd like to be a volunteer.' I'll select three or four, take them into some seminars or Sunday evening services at the prison and see how they react after a few hours of exposure to prison life. Often, that's it and they don't come back. But sometimes one person will come out of the group to be a continuing volunteer."

Other qualities are important, too. Harry Howard, chaplain at San Quentin, looks for a well-grounded, well-rounded person. "An effective volunteer is one who is mature—not a new Christian—and well-grounded in the faith. He should be able to talk about his Christian life in religious language or nonreligious language, but he should also be able to talk about other things as well—world events, sports, whatever the inmate is interested in. After all, we're there not to talk about what *we* want to talk about but what that inmate is experiencing and what his problems are."

Knowing the Bible is important for the Christian volunteer, says Chaplain Wagner. "We tell the inmates in our prison Bible study groups that they can ask any question they want on life, death, heaven, hell, or eternity, and we try to answer on the basis of the Bible. We need volunteers who have a decent working knowledge of the Bible, but who are also willing to say, 'I don't know but I'll find out.' "

Proper motivation is critical for the Christian volunteer. Larry Mathre, a regional administrator for the Federal Bureau of Prisons, observes, "So many people envision chaplaincy and jail ministry as simply preaching and evangelizing; they don't always seem to have the concern for the individual inmate in mind." Along this line Chaplain Craig comments, "Many times a person comes to the prison as a volunteer because he simply wants to report back to his church on the number of souls 'saved' or whatever. Certainly souls are a concern, but I feel you grow Christians like you grow a garden. It takes time and patience. Are you going to be around to follow up or are you just 'counting heads?' "

In agreement is Don Severson, chaplain at the federal correctional institution at Lompoc, California, who says, "We have had very few failures among volunteers, but the ones who have failed have usually been those who try to 'hit the inmate over the head' with the Bible."

THE THREE KEY QUALITIES

I think there are three keys to being an effective Christian volunteer in a prison or jail: proper motivation, commitment, and preparation. If any of these keys is inadequate or missing, you won't find the fulfilling ministry God has for you.

Motivation

Having the right motivation is fundamental. People volunteer for many reasons—some noble, some shabby. Among prison and jail volunteers there are those who come to fulfill a personal need or desire. With some, there is a subtle "need to be needed." Others have the idea that prison work is exciting or glamorous; they want to see the "dangerous criminals" behind bars. (Inmates caustically refer to this sort of person as being on a "zoo trip.") Some volunteers have a desire for the approval of others, or they want to reform the penal system. Some simply want to proselytize or be able to report numbers of persons "witnessed to" or "saved."

A study of jail volunteers in Denver showed three principal reasons for their involvement: humanitarianism, an interest in corrections, and a sense of community responsibility.[1] Another study, this one of volunteers in four prisons in Canada, listed the major motivations of volunteers as personal interest, encouragement by some other person or group, their perceptions of the needs of inmates, interest in corrections, humanitarianism, or a feeling of having "something to offer."[2]

I believe that the only lasting and honest motive for a Christian must be obedience to Christ, including the desire to see Him honored and the wish to meet the needs of inmates in a sensitive, caring way. Before you begin to work with inmates, ask yourself some searching questions:

- Can I honestly accept people like inmates, who are so different from myself in background and values?
- What are my prejudices concerning such people?
- Do I really believe God can change the inner direction of a person's life—even a habitual criminal or a drug addict?
- Am I willing to continue to minister to inmates, even in the face of rejection? Can I and will I pray for inmates?
- Am I really seeking the praise of men or the glory of God?

When you know the answers to these questions and see that those answers point toward prison or jail work, then you should consider becoming involved.

Commitment

The next key to effective volunteer work in prisons is commitment. This ministry is not for the casual, the hurried, or the fainthearted. Many chaplains have remarked on the high dropout rate among would-be volunteers. The first ninety days seem to be the critical period. One chaplain suggested that anyone wanting to do prison work should plan weekly visits for a year. "It will take him six months just to learn his way around." While that may be a slight exaggeration, there is no doubt that becoming familiar with the prison environment, the rules, and learning how to relate to inmates will take time and effort. Perhaps agreeing to a fixed period of involvement would be a useful way to start.

What really hurts is when a volunteer fails to "count the cost." Paul Markstrom writes, "There are many who would want to become involved in the religious volunteer program but who, for various reasons, would find such involvement most painful, threatening, and would finally find some excuse for not continuing."[3] Volunteers who start and then quit demoralize the inmate, disappoint the chaplain and the prison staff, and give a bad image to the efforts of the church. Consistency, persistency, and patience are the primary virtues of a committed volunteer.

Preparation

The third key for the effective volunteer is personal preparation. This starts, I believe, with soul-searching prayer that seeks answers to questions like: Is this a ministry I should explore further? Do I see the need and feel a burden for those in prison? Preparation also includes a good knowledge of basic Christianity and how to use the Bible effectively. Most inmates are not concerned with the finer points of theology or denominational distinctives, but they do want to hear a clear message of Jesus Christ crucified, risen, and living today with power in the lives of His followers.

You should also feel comfortable in one-to-one casual conversation or in small groups, because these are frequent situations for prison workers. Just because you are considered a good Sunday school teacher or a pretty fair preacher is no sign you can be effective in prison or jail ministries. The communication methods are often much different.

Another part of your preparation is a general understanding of the correctional system and of the way in which Christian volunteer ministries can be carried out within that system. This book is just a start. You should read more (see Chapter 11 for some suggestions) and talk with other people who have done this type of ministry. Try to get a feel for what is involved and what may be required of you. Detailed orientation and specific training will often come from the chaplain of the prison (if that is where you begin your volunteer work). In situations where there is no chaplain, try to work with another experienced volunteer (that's always the best way to start, in any situation). The institution's administrator also will tell you about the do's and don'ts of his institution.

STAGES IN VOLUNTEER ATTITUDES

Reverend Markstrom, in his manual on volunteers in prison religious programs, reports that most volunteers go through several stages if they continue in this ministry.[4] The first stage, he says, is one of "a high degree of motivation along with the accompanying somewhat 'starry-eyed' posture. . . . Often in the new volunteer there may be a deep feeling of pity and sympathy for the incarcerated person. This sympathy may be fueled by reports the inmate may be supplying." Some volunteers may even have an inflated view of themselves, thinking that they are just what the inmate—and the correctional system—needs to accomplish a change for the better. The subtle dangers of pride!

The second stage Markstrom sees is one marked by feelings of anger at the prison system and a zealousness to change things. In part, these feelings are the natural result of wanting to be helpful and constructive, but they may also result from the volunteer's failure to understand how the prison system works and the purposes of the staff and administration. This is a stage when it is important not to judge but to try to learn more and understand what is happening.

Finally, the volunteer will probably reach a point where he has gained some objectivity about the prison system, about himself, and about his relationships with inmates and with staff. He has become accustomed to the prison conditions without necessarily condoning or accepting them, and he can see the strengths as well as the weaknesses in the people he meets in the prison or jail where he is working. Being able to regularly share his feelings and experiences with other volunteers and with a chaplain can be of great help in reaching this level in his effectiveness.

"DO'S" AND "DON'TS" OF PRISON MINISTRY

To be an effective volunteer you will have to know some principles and guidelines for this type of ministry. There are some "absolutes" that any would-be volunteer must know and understand if he is to work within a prison or jail program. Most of these principles and guidelines revolve around the security of the institution, the relationship with the inmates, and the nature of the volunteer's personal witness. All are intended to insure that your Christian testimony is clear and your ministry effective.

Follow the Rules

The cardinal rule of prison and jail ministry is to obey all the rules of the institution. You are a guest in someone else's house, so come as a guest. Recognize that each institution is a highly structured community and that security is a primary consideration. Chaplain Wagner of Cook County Jail emphasizes, "A good volunteer will *follow every rule* in the institution. The rule may seem stupid, but he's happy to submit himself to every rule. One volunteer can ruin a whole program and bring it to an end by not doing this."

When in Doubt, Ask

There will be many things you will not understand at first, and even after you have been involved in prison or jail for a while you will encounter new situations. Never assume anything; ask questions of those in authority. This will often be the chaplain, because he is responsible for your being there and his personal effectiveness is at stake. If there is no chaplain, ask the responsible prison or jail official with whom you have been working. If you are working under a leader of a team of volunteers, ask the leader.

Take Nothing in—Take Nothing Out

Do not take anything into a prison to give to an inmate nor take anything from an inmate to take out without the explicit permission of the chaplain or responsible jail official. Even seemingly innocent things can cause great difficulties. In federal prisons, for example, "contraband" is defined as "any article which is unauthorized under the circumstances and includes, but is not limited to, the following: letters, stamps, tools, weapons, food, implements, messages and instruments." A stick of gum can be used to make a compression mold of a lock. A simple request to "mail this letter to my mother so it will go out faster" could actually be part of a blackmail effort. Don't distribute tracts or literature without the chaplain's approval. Many inmates will try to "con" volunteers and "use" them, so caution is always the rule. You can always say, "I'll have to ask the chaplain about that."

See Inmates as Individuals

Each man and woman in prison has unique experiences,

feelings, and desires. Look at that person with whom you are talking as you would anyone else. Don't make assumptions based upon generalities or stereotypes. A training manual for small groups says, "The most important thing anyone who works in a prison ministry can remember is that inmates have the same basic feelings, needs, and expectations as has the outsider."[5] Jesus taught groups, but He cared for individuals.

Keep Your Objectivity

You will have to struggle with this for a while; you want to be able to listen to the inmate with understanding, but at the same time appreciate the situation of the prison or jail officials, the needs of the chaplain, and your own role as a Christian volunteer. If you become too wrapped up in the needs of the inmate you will lose credibility with the administrators and quite possibly lose your access to the institution. Remember your primary motivation.

Be Willing To Learn

You don't know it all so don't go into prison with that attitude. Be willing to learn from the chaplain; accept his leadership and recognize his insights. Be willing to learn from the inmates. They have seen a side of life you may never have encountered. If an inmate is a Christian, he may have insights and perspectives on Scripture that will broaden your own understanding.

Be Dependable

This is critically important, as the earlier comments of chaplains emphasized. Inmates have known so many broken promises in life that they hardly expect anyone to be dependable. If you say you are going to come on a certain day, be there. Don't make promises you can't keep. Chaplain Wagner points to the need for dependability: "Dependability—the volunteer who is there week after week—really impresses inmates." Chaplain Howard at San Quentin has one volunteer who has been coming for twenty-seven years! Your consistency is part of your Christian witness.

Be Patient

Prison and jail work is a long, slow process. One experienced volunteer described it as a "marathon race." You will be working with people whose lives have been shaped and warped by years of highly negative influences. It will take time and patience to have a positive effect on some people. Just remember that the inmate has an "enforced patience," while you can seek yours from God.

Be a Good Listener

Many inmates have never had anyone seriously listen to them and really *hear* them. Perhaps the most valuable gift you can bring to an inmate is the quality of being a good listener. By "good" I mean non-judgmental and understanding (although not always believing or accepting everything told you). Be willing to help the inmate find the right questions to ask before you rush in with "answers," even Christian ones.

Be Honest

Chaplain Silber comments that for some reason prisoners "have the uncanny ability to read whether or not you are honest."[6] Inmates are very sensitive to hypocrisy, to phonies, to people who try to "play games" with them. As a Christian, honesty is particularly vital; your life and your words had better match up.

Don't Come As Expert or Reformer

Reading this book or ten others won't make you an expert on corrections or on the problems of the penal system. Don't come in to tell the prison officials or the jailers how to do their jobs. If you decide your primary desire is to reform the system, find some other channel to express that desire; don't do it through the religious program or under the guise of Christian witness.

Don't Come To Help Yourself

Chaplain Silber makes this point: "If you have problems or if you have needs, then deal with those problems and those needs before you come to us, because we need all of your loving, all of your caring, all of you. We need you as whole as you possibly can be because we are living with people who are not whole, who are torn asunder, who are shredded apart."[7] In the words of Jesus, "The Son of man also came not to be served but to serve . . ." (Mark 10:45, RSV).

Be Prepared

Prison and jail ministry, like any work for God, deserves your best. Never settle for an offhand, ill-prepared involvement. Being prepared is part of being a good ambassador for Jesus. If you are to lead a Bible class, know your material thoroughly and how to present it. If you are to give a testimony or sing a song, rehearse it ahead of time so it can be done smoothly. Be on time to your commitments. Dress appropriately when visiting prisoners, neither shabbily nor formally. You are seeking to love and care for others in such a way that they will not be distracted by you, but rather will see Jesus.

Be a Christian

I am writing to Christians, not to people with simply a humanitarian concern. Come into a prison or jail ministry with the spiritual distinctive that should mark the follower of Jesus. You have something and Someone unique to present. Don't dilute your witness by trying to be different things. Chaplain Silber says, "You are a Christian; your desire is to share the love of Christ with another person in a caring relationship under some difficult circumstances. If you can convey this, then you have done more than anybody else has been able to do in whatever length of life the person has already experienced. You are coming because you are *being* to them *Love.* You are coming because you are *being* to them *Christ.*"[8]

The work of Christian volunteers in prisons and jails demands a high standard. Not everyone is suited to it. It requires a dedication and a commitment that can come only from the Spirit of Christ as you lay yourself open to His working in your life. Your ministry may be within prison walls, with offenders on parole, counseling with juveniles, or in the ministries of prayer and correspondence from your home. Whatever opportunity you find before you, take it with the Lord's help, carry it out to His glory, and the commendation will truly be yours, "Well done, good and faithful servant."

CHAPTER 7 REVIEW QUESTIONS

1. Consistency and dependability are essential qualities of a prison volunteer.
   a) True.
   b) False.

2. A Christian prison volunteer should be motivated by a desire to
   a) win souls.
   b) obey Christ.
   c) demonstrate his faith.
   d) reform the prison system.

3. If the prison volunteer sees no results of his efforts after a few visits, he probably should seek some other area of ministry.
   a) True.
   b) False.

4. A person who is a good preacher or Sunday school teacher will also be a good prison volunteer.
   a) True.
   b) Not necessarily true.
   c) False.

5. Prison volunteers go through stages of personal feelings toward the prison system and understanding of their role.
   a) True.
   b) False.

6. The absolutely fundamental rule of prison and jail ministry is
   a) follow all regulations and procedures.
   b) never hesitate to ask questions.
   c) take nothing in or out of the prison.
   d) None of the above.

7. "Being a good listener" primarily means
   a) looking for the opening in a conversation that will allow you to present the gospel.
   b) seeking to understand the person's real desires, interests, and needs, and responding to these as appropriate.
   c) waiting to speak until the other person is finished talking.

8. Becoming a church prison volunteer is a good way to discover how prisons and jails can be improved.
   a) Yes, definitely.
   b) No, because your activities are too limited.
   c) Perhaps, but that should never be your motive.

9. When is it permitted to give an inmate a gift or small favor?
   a) Never.
   b) Only with the permission of the chaplain or jailer.
   c) Whenever such gifts or favors would promote the inmate-volunteer relationship.

10. When working with an inmate, a volunteer should
    a) try to determine which category of prisoner the inmate fits.
    b) view the inmate as a unique individual.
    c) assume that most inmates have similar characteristics.

8

Caring for the Families of Inmates

As Corrie ten Boom and I were visiting the huge prison at San Quentin, talking together of the needs and problems of prisoners, something she said struck me. "The families are the ones who often suffer the most." With her sensitivity to the human needs around us, she had focused on one of the forgotten elements of prison ministry. A Missouri state chaplain echoed Corrie's remark when he said, "Most if not all of the emphasis is placed on the welfare of the inmate, and very little attention has been paid to the problems and heartaches of the wives, mothers, children, and families."

Several hundred thousand families are directly affected every year by having one of their loved ones in a prison or jail. This is a traumatic experience that can either shatter a family or, with love and attention from caring people, bring the family together to be a source of strength to the one in prison.

The prison ministry guide for one denomination summarizes well the problems of the families of inmates: "Few families of prisoners receive enough attention from the churches. Most of these families are broken, torn by strife and tension, generally disrupted, and filled with a great amount of anxiety. Many families experience extreme financial problems, in part because there is little knowledge of budgeting income. Others often cannot help themselves because, like the prisoner, the wives and children lack employable skills. Medical problems, bills, housing problems, and children difficult to control are common. Legal problems, including pending divorce actions, are to be expected."[1] This is not a pretty picture, and it is made worse by the social stigma attached to a family that has a member in prison.

Studies have shown that a family that can stay together and keep in touch with the member in prison will have an important influence in helping that member readjust successfully to society. Studies by Lloyd Ohlin and Douglas Glaser showed that prisoners who had an active correspondence (that is, received two or more letters a month from relatives) were noticeably more successful on parole than inmates who had little or no continuing correspondence.

Most inmates with families are anxious for their family's welfare and frustrated at not being able to help. A study of prisoners and their families at the Illinois State Penitentiary revealed that in most writings of prisoners (letters, prisoner newspapers, and magazines), themes of "deep concern for the well-being of their families, despair at the separation, and resentment toward the justice system and society for imposing this forced separation" occur again and again.[2] "I haven't heard from my wife" or "My husband hasn't written in a month" are typical and frequent comments from both sides of the prison walls.

When a family member (usually the husband) is arrested, the suddenness often creates great anxiety, fear, and uncertainty for the wife, children, and parents. What will happen? How can the husband be contacted? Does he need anything? Can we do anything? What about bail, a lawyer, and money to pay for them? The point has been well made that imprisonment brings a double crisis to a family. First is the crisis of demoralization, the fact that one of the family members has been arrested for breaking some law. The second crisis is that the family is split apart. Losing a family member to imprisonment is similar to the person being killed, except that he will probably eventually return.

When the husband is arrested, the wife often does not receive enough information about what has happened to know what to do. Immediately following the arrest, the husband may be out of reach for hours or even days. Later, visiting time is limited and privacy impossible. The wife is anxious and worried, the situation may be difficult to explain to the children, tensions can develop with parents, and there may not be anyone around to ask for help. Wives and other family members need support and encouragement during any court visits or trials. It is a great strain to sit and watch a loved one go through court proceedings. For a wife or parents to face this ordeal alone can be unbearable.

For wives, the immediate need is usually for information: information about the husband's status, when and how to visit the prison or jail, and how to get help from various social services (legal, welfare, child care, etc.). The next biggest concern is often for money. Many families find themselves with limited funds or are unable even to buy food. Welfare funds take time to arrive; meanwhile, the family may be in great financial need.

Later as the reality of imprisonment becomes settled, wives may need someone to help them make the many adjustments demanded by the new situation. An understanding listener during this time will become a much-appreciated friend and counselor.

LOVING THE LOVED ONES ON THE OUTSIDE

You can see that churches and individual Christians have many opportunities to demonstrate practical love and caring for families in this situation. Simply being there and being available is important. A wife will be greatly encouraged by knowing there are some people who are concerned about her and who are willing to help.

Volunteers can help the wife and family find out about available services. Helping the wife find a job (if that is needed) or providing child care are two important ways to assist. Some churches have emergency funds that can be made available to help a family temporarily until other income can be arranged.

Provide Rides to the Prison

Many prisons (and some jails) are not conveniently located to transportation routes. Getting to the prison for a visit can pose a real problem for an inmate's wife. Even if the wife is traveling from out of town and can reach the nearest community by bus, schedules are often inconvenient and taxi fares high. Volunteers can provide transportation to the prison or jail as a tangible way of caring for an inmate's family. The drive to the prison can also provide an opportunity to get acquainted and to develop friendships. You can learn how the family needs help. You may find an opportunity to share your faith. Especially where a long drive is involved, a husband-and-wife team or two women volunteers should go together. This is important both for propriety and to allow one partner to drive while the other gets acquainted with the family. Church members can take turns providing this transportation while other volunteers provide child care as needed.

Provide Places To Stay—Hospitality

Another way of showing care to the families of inmates is through providing temporary accommodations for them if they have come from out of town to visit at the prison or jail. Wives may travel hundreds of miles to be able to have a brief visit with their husbands, and many do not have money for hotels or motels. Some churches may be able to provide such accommodations. Another approach, used in a growing number of communities, is to have a central "hospitality house" which can provide for transportation, child care, meals, and sometimes temporary rooms. In some communities, churches have cooperated to start such a ministry or to support an existing one.

A typical hospitality house would provide information and referral to various community services for welfare, food, housing, and employment. It would coordinate volunteers to provide regular transportation to the various prisons and jails in the area, perhaps within a range of several hundred miles. Regular meals (perhaps supplied by local churches or other groups) are available. Child care is provided so that wives need not worry about their children while visiting. The staff of a hospitality house may also provide personal counseling.

Typically, a hospitality house may have one or two paid staff members who are assisted by volunteers. Funding may come from contributions of local churches and civic organizations and from governmental sources, such as grants from the Law Enforcement Assistance Administration. Hospitality houses offer a highly satisfying and tangible way for Christians to assist families of inmates.

A wife may also be encouraged to take part in the church fellowship. This is something to be approached tactfully without pushing, but if church members can make the wife and children feel truly welcome this will go toward encouraging the family to remain together and to support the husband in prison. Later, if the family remains in the local area after the husband is released, the witness and fellowship of the church can be important in helping the husband make a successful adjustment to society.

A chaplain from Idaho wrote to me, "We can't stress too much that the family is desperately in need of Christian love." I believe that local churches and individual Christians can have an impact for Christ far beyond what they thought possible—simply through consistent, caring Christian love for the wives and families of those in prison.

CHAPTER 8 REVIEW QUESTIONS

1. Most prisons and jails have no programs for helping families of inmates.
   a) True.
   b) False.

2. When a family member goes to jail or prison, he or she can be helped best if
   a) other family members stay in touch.
   b) all contact is stopped or greatly limited during the time in confinement.
   c) only one family member is the point of contact.

3. Writing letters to inmates is not helpful because it is a painful reminder of the free world.
   a) True.
   b) False.

4. The major concerns of a family with one member in prison are
   a) lack of information about the inmate's status.
   b) family finances.
   c) coping with social stigma.
   d) All of the above.
   e) b) and c).

5. Since there are public welfare agencies or hospitality houses, churches need not be concerned about inmates' families visiting at prisons or jails.
   a) True.
   b) False.

6. The family of an inmate should be tactfully invited to be part of a church fellowship even if they don't want to become church members.
   a) True.
   b) False.

7. Families of persons just arrested tend to "pull together" during the crisis period and therefore don't need help from outsiders.
   a) Not always.
   b) Usually.

8. Immediately after a family member is arrested, Christian volunteers should
   a) wait a while before offering to help, so the family will not resent an intrusion into their privacy.
   b) offer assistance, because the family needs emotional and practical support.
   c) notify appropriate social welfare agencies.

9. If a wife wants to visit her husband at a prison or jail, one of the most helpful services to provide her with is
   a) money.
   b) transportation.
   c) literature.
   d) directions to the jail or prison.

10. While helping the family of an inmate, Christian volunteers should
    a) not directly witness to the family, as this is taking advantage of the family's distress.
    b) witness to family members openly and as soon as possible.
    c) allow a clear witness to grow naturally and tactfully out of the situation.

9

The Local Church in Prison Ministries

Every other Saturday, laymen from the Parkwood Baptist Church in Jacksonville, Florida, embark on what they call a "prison regeneration program." Groups of men travel to the nearby state prison, the prison farm, the county jail, and a work release center to conduct worship services, visit with inmates, and talk about a personal relationship with Jesus Christ.

This program developed from the concern of two of the church's laymen and one of the chaplains at the state prison, and began as a follow-up ministry to an evangelistic crusade held at the prison. The visitation program is now supported by a Bible correspondence course program, sponsored by the church, with almost two hundred inmates enrolled, as well as a cassette tape ministry in which inmates are provided tape players and access to a tape library of Christian teaching and preaching.

Parkwood Church is but one example of what churches of all denominations in many parts of the country are doing to reach through the walls and bars of prisons and jails with the words and love of Jesus Christ. The tremendous fact of prison ministry is that it is an opportunity near at hand. Every community has at least a jail. Many have other correctional institutions, such as halfway houses, detention centers, and prisons. A church that is interested in prisoners doesn't have to look far.

It is this nearness that is also part of the shameful neglect by churches for prison ministries. Between 1,500 and 2,000 jails have no religious services for inmates. Many of these are small or medium-sized, but a few have several hundred inmates. Many detention centers, work farms, and other institutions also lack a consistent Christian witness. Too many churches are unaware of this need or, regrettably, have turned aside from it. Yet every church can do *something* for prisoners. Mickey Parrish, an active layman in the Parkwood Church's prison ministry, said he never felt "called" to a prison ministry. "The Scriptures plainly tell us we ought to visit those in prison, so we ought to just go and do it, and not wait for God to call us in some mysterious way."[1]

"LORD, WHAT WILL YOU HAVE ME TO DO?"

That was Paul's question to Jesus on the Damascus road and that should be your question too. By now you have learned something about the needs of prisoners and the possibilities for a Christian ministry to them. You have seen what Scripture teaches and what our Lord commands of His followers. What is your next step?

It is *not* to decide yes or no about prison ministries—not yet.

First Step: Investigate

Right now you need to know more about the situation in your community before you can pray intelligently or make an informed decision. What you need to do first, either alone or together with someone else who shares your concern, is to investigate. Talk with other members in your church to see what they know about prison ministries or the needs in your community. Contact the local ministerial association to see what programs it sponsors or what it believes the needs to be for prison work. Look in your telephone directory under your community government for a listing for the local jail, or under "U.S. Government" for a listing of any federal correctional facilities. Telephone and ask for the chaplain or the person who coordinates religious programs for the inmates. Find out what programs are being provided and what other needs there are.

Perhaps you or someone in your church knows one of the local judges or court officials. Talk with these people to see what programs they know about for offender rehabilitation or assistance, and where they think volunteers could be helpful. Look for agencies such as halfway houses, juvenile detention centers, and prisoner's aid organizations. A few well-placed telephone calls can reveal a wealth of information about programs and agencies in your town or city that are working with offenders.

Here are some questions to be answered in your search:

- Where are the institutions in this community that hold prisoners?
- What programs already exist for the caring of prisoners?
- What are the needs for volunteer programs as seen by prison or jail officials?
- What appear to be the needs of prisoners, particularly for spiritual nurture and guidance?
- How can families of inmates be contacted? Where do they live? What are their needs?
- Do lower courts (handling misdemeanors) have alternatives to jail or bail? Would the judge accept church people as probation sponsors for juveniles?
- What people in the church are already involved in some type of prison or jail ministry, and which ones have expressed interest?

Second Step: Evaluate

Now take the information you have gathered and sort it out. Where are the needs that might be met by volunteers? Where are religious programs provided and where are they not? What seem to be the attitudes of the various officials and administrators you talked with? How open are they to volunteer programs in general? What other Christian agencies, groups, churches, or individuals are already at work in prisons and jails?

Next, think about what you and your church might *consistently* do if you were to become involved in a prison ministry. It is better to start small and let the ministry grow slowly than to try to begin a large effort that will soon fail for lack of interest and support. Consider what activities of a general humanitarian nature you could provide, and what activities of a specifically spiritual nature would be possible. Just don't start a prison ministry with the idea of trying to save the whole jail or prison. Be concerned with discipleship and Christian growth as well as evangelism.

Also recognize that some activities and ministries are appropriate at different times: during imprisonment, after release, helping prisoners' families, and providing alternatives to imprisonment. Here is a list of some things you might consider:

- visiting inmates
- providing or assisting with worship services
- providing special musical programs
- conducting Bible studies
- starting or supporting small sharing groups
- one-to-one counseling
- providing literature, tapes, films
- providing a Bible correspondence course
- teaching classes in a specific skill, trade, or in personal adjustment
- leading recreation programs
- corresponding with inmates
- acting as sponsor for someone on parole or probation
- locating jobs for ex-offenders
- arranging for temporary housing
- providing pre-release information services
- helping inmates' families stay in touch, especially through visits
- providing referral and information for families of prisoners

- involving prisoners' families in church fellowship
- organizing prayer groups in the church
- finding specific ways to support and encourage chaplains

These are some of the ways you as an individual Christian and your church as a group of believers can become involved in a ministry to prisoners. As you explore the situation in your community you will probably discover other ways as well.

Third Step: Pray

Now you are ready to pray. You are attacking a stronghold of Satan, so lay a foundation of prayer before you begin. Knowing the needs and knowing some specific things that you and others might do, you are ready to pray about what God would have you do. Review what the Bible says about the needs of prisoners and about the kinds of service required of every Christian. Pray earnestly and specifically that God would make it clear to you and others *whether* this is the ministry you should become involved with and, if so, *what* He would have you do. Enlist other Christians to pray with you and be persistent in your prayers until you agree together on what should be done. (For information on how to start a prayer group, write to Christian Prison Volunteers. See Chapter 11.)

Fourth Step: Prepare

If you find that God has shown you areas of prison ministry you believe you can work in, then begin the preparation. Perhaps you will have found one or two other Christians who share your concern and who are willing to become involved. In addition, arrange for other Christians to be praying regularly for your efforts. Still others may be able to help by obtaining materials, beginning correspondence with inmates, or providing transportation. Not everyone need be involved inside the walls.

Fifth Step: Act

Contact the chaplain or official at the institution where you believe you can be the greatest help. Discuss with him what and how you and others can be involved. Be willing to take his direction and counsel. Arrange for some orientation to the institution as a first step in developing interest and (as often happens) in "weeding out" those persons who feel uncomfortable with this type of ministry.

Within the church, hold orientation sessions with the core of potential volunteers, perhaps seeing a film on prisons, reading materials on prison work, and discussing principles of effective prison volunteerism (as I have suggested in Chapter 7). Use this as a time to explore personal motivations and to study the biblical basis of your ministry. Make sure every volunteer clearly understands what your ministry is and what its limitations are. Then come to the institution's chaplain or administrator for more detailed guidance before actually beginning your work. (Formalized training in prison ministry is conducted by Christian Prison Volunteers. Write for current information, dates, and places; see Chapter 11.)

Recognize that much of your ministry, particularly in jails, often allows little time to develop mature Christians. Prisons have a more stable population and you may see results from consistent and faithful ministry. But don't become discouraged when you don't see immediate or lasting changes in some prisoners. Be faithful and let God bring the increase.

One approach to a visitation-counseling ministry is to have teams of volunteers who report to a volunteer coordinator. This person provides communication with the jail or prison administrators, answers questions from volunteers, and gets information from the institution. Volunteer teams should plan to meet together prior to visiting an institution and then again following the visit, so they can share problems, questions, and good experiences. Volunteers working in teams can encourage and support one another and are likely to be more effective than individual volunteers working alone.

Let me summarize how you can begin a prison or jail ministry:

- *Investigate:* Find out what's being done or not done in your community.
- *Understand:* Review and analyze what you've learned to see what's needed.
- *Reflect:* What could *you* and *your church* do?
- *Pray:* Enlist others to pray with you.
- *Prepare:* Get others involved, gather materials, make plans.
- *Begin:* Start small and slowly.
- *Cooperate:* Work closely with prison and jail officials.
- *Continue:* Commit yourself to the ministry, be consistent, and stick with it.

The mechanics of starting a prison or jail ministry are not difficult. The difficulty comes with the initial awareness and with accepting a concern for prisoners as a biblical mandate and a ministry that is within the reach of almost any local church. In many communities, if the local churches do not take the initiative to establish and maintain a Christian witness in the jails and prisons, it will not happen at all. The church is not a refuge from the world; it is a training ground for people who will faithfully care and serve those in the world who are so much in need of the love and grace of Jesus Christ. In the prisons and jails of America are hundreds of thousands of people who very much want to hear of that love and grace. I hope the reply of your heart is that of the prophet Isaiah: "Here am I; send me."

CHAPTER 9 REVIEW QUESTIONS

1. Since so many humanitarian organizations have become active in the criminal justice system, there is less place for work by individual churches.
   a) True.
   b) False.

2. A church's first step in getting into a local prison ministry is to make a firm commitment to begin such a work.
   a) True.
   b) False.

3. Information on local prison and jail needs for religious ministries can be found by
   a) contacting the local ministerial association.
   b) calling or visiting local jail or prison officials.
   c) talking with other people in your church.
   d) all of the above.

4. If other churches have prison programs, the best thing is to set up your own church's program so inmates and chaplains will recognize your individuality.
   a) True.
   b) Not necessarily true.
   c) Never should be the case.

5. To be effective, a church should plan to start a jail or prison ministry slowly and with a small number of committed people.
   a) True.
   b) False.

6. There are only a few specific ministries churches can do well in prison and jail ministries, and these should be emphasized.
   a) True.
   b) False.

7. A church that is starting a prison ministry should have its own orientation program even if the jail or prison has one.
   a) True.
   b) False.

8. The primary orientation and preparation needed by most prison volunteers consists of
   a) knowledge of the Bible, training in techniques of witnessing, and personal prayer.
   b) knowledge of prison or jail procedures and characteristics of the inmates.
   c) lectures by the prison staff and reading of books on prisons.
   d) All of the above.

9. Where possible, prison volunteers should
   a) work individually.
   b) work as teams under a pastor or coordinator.
   c) work only with persons of the same sex.

10. All persons wanting to be part of a prison ministry must share their faith inside a prison or jail.
   a) True.
   b) False.

10

Answering Your Questions

"I'm interested in prison ministry, but . . ."

By now you probably have some questions about volunteer work in prisons and jails. You may be interested but yet feel uncertain or apprehensive. Is this a ministry you could really do? What about all those terrible things you've heard about prisons?

Let me try to respond to some of the common questions volunteers seem to have about prison ministry. It is my hope that these answers will help to clear your own thoughts and allow you to pray more specifically about what God would have you do.

Isn't prison work dangerous?

Not as much as you might think, despite the television dramas or the occasional newspaper account of a prison disturbance. In fact, you probably have more to fear from an automobile accident while driving to the prison or jail than from anything that might happen to you while at the institution. Certainly there is some element of risk, but remember that you will be at an institution for only a few hours a month; the prison staff are there all day every day. Follow the rules and the leadership of the chaplain and you will be all right.

I'd feel awkward talking to a prisoner. What do I say?

What do you say to anyone when you first meet him? Remember, you will be talking to people who have many of the same fears, interests, and concerns as you have. Look for areas of common interest. If you are part of a specific activity, such as a Bible study or a correspondence course, that activity can be a focus of your conversation at first. Then as you explore shared interests or as you listen with understanding to the other person, you will find plenty to talk about. At some point the inmate will want to know why you are there and what motivates you. That will be an opportunity to tactfully share your Christian motivation and to learn how the inmate views his own spiritual needs.

What do I do if the local jailer doesn't want a prison religious program?

This will be a rare situation, so try to find out the real reason. Some jailers have had bad experiences in the past and will be hesitant to let volunteers into the jail. Explain specifically what your church or group has in mind. Try to get the jail staff involved in planning this ministry so they will be comfortable with the results and will see that it will not cause them unusual problems. Start small; don't ask to have large groups come in at first, just two or three trained and committed people. If you will be the leader of the volunteers from your church, let the jailer know you will always be available to him to answer questions and handle problems.

Meanwhile, pray and explore other avenues of ministry as well. Perhaps a correspondence program ("visit by mail") or caring for families of inmates is possible. Look to the courts and juvenile halls for potential ministry areas. Ask some judges for their suggestions. And in all of this, look for existing programs. Instead of duplicating what others are doing, you want to reinforce them where possible.

I'm not able to visit prisons or jails, but I'd like to help. What can I do?

There is much you can do. Prayer is the need often mentioned by chaplains. Pray for chaplains, for volunteers, for Christian inmates, for opportunities to talk with inmates, and for the provision of materials such as literature or cassette tapes. You can encourage other Christians to volunteer. They may not be aware of the needs or the opportunities. By telephone, letter, and personal meeting, you may be able to enlist others for this important ministry.

And you can visit inmates by mail. Prisoners eagerly look forward to receiving mail, yet many get little or none. Become a "prison pen pal" to one or several prisoners. You can encourage them with positive letters, birthday cards, and helpful literature. Visiting by mail can be one of the most rewarding and satisfying ministries you can undertake. A call or letter to the chaplain or administrator at a nearby prison or jail can get you started.

I'm a young single woman and would like to help, but I'm not sure what I can do.

Many chaplains and jailers have reservations about single women as visitors or counselors of male inmates. Many young women are active, however, as prison volunteers in several ways. You can have a significant ministry with women inmates. Women in jails and prisons are often overlooked, yet they too are much in need of friendship, counseling, and a Christian witness. You may be able to be an effective counselor to young people, both male and female, who have been released on probation.

Within prisons or jails you may be able to work as a team member with other volunteers, perhaps a married couple. Outside the prison you can work with others from your church in caring for the families of inmates—providing transportation for a wife to the prison or jail, taking children on an outing, and showing Christ's love for them in many other ways. "Visiting by mail" can also be an effective ministry for you. Many inmates enjoy corresponding with young ladies and would welcome the opportunity to exchange letters with you.

As a pastor, what can I do to encourage interest in my congregation for prison and jail ministry?

Start by visiting local jails or prisons, talking with the chaplain or administrator, and learning what their needs are. Have in mind what members of your congregation might be able to do, but go with the idea of finding out what is needed and where you might fit. Identify one or two key lay people in your congregation who could be interested in this ministry and who could form the core and leadership for other volunteers. Get them involved and trained (formalized training is available through the Association of Christian Prison Workers; see Chapter 11), and support them as they work to get others involved. Look for local halfway houses or hospitality houses that care for families of inmates; see if there are ways your church can help. Perhaps there is nothing of this sort in your community; should your church (alone or together with others) begin such ministries? Include illustrations and examples in your sermons describing the needs of prisoners and the potential for prison ministries. Make available to your congregations books, articles, and brochures that describe prison ministries. Schedule films for use in evening services or adult Sunday school classes.

I could visit but I'm not a trained counselor. Suppose an inmate appears to have emotional or other problems I can't deal with. What can I do?

As part of your orientation to a prison or large jail, you should ask about the other professional services that are available. A prison staff may include parole officers, a psychiatrist, or a social service case worker, and these people are responsible for helping inmates with problems. You should discuss an inmate's apparent need with the chaplain and let him make the necessary referral. In jails, the noncorrectional professional staff is limited or nonexistent, and you would have to talk with the jail staff or, preferably, the volunteer coordinator.

From what I've read about jails and prisons, I think more should be done to reform and change the correctional system. How is caring for inmates going to achieve that?

Directly, it won't. Remember, there are two basic motivations for volunteers in prison work: reform the system or help the inmates. You must decide at the start which is your basic concern and not let the two be mixed. If you want to work for prison reform, fine, but don't do it under the pretense of being a representative of Christ coming to care for inmates. The Christian volunteer who desires to share Christ's love with inmates is not seeking to change policies or tell the prison administration how to do its job. The volunteer is to be an "agent of change" to help the inmate move from being self-directed to being Christ-directed. Focus clearly on that role and you won't become confused with those working for reform.

There are many inmates from minority ethnic groups. What is being done for them?

Not as much as could be done. In some jails and prisons, persons of black or Hispanic background are in the majority; in some areas American Indians may be among the inmates. To have Christian volunteers who are themselves of a minority background is desirable, but as several chaplains have emphasized, the quality of the volunteer's Christian commitment is more important than the ethnic background. What is sometimes needed are volunteers who speak the foreign language of many inmates (Spanish, for example) or Christian literature in an appropriate language.

Where can I get more information about prison ministries?

I'm glad you asked that question, because now I can refer you to Chapter 11, which lists and describes some of the resources that will tell you more about the challenging ministry to those in prisons and jails.

CHAPTER 10 REVIEW QUESTIONS

1 Prison work is dangerous for volunteers
   a) at all times.
   b) occasionally.
   c) in large prisons only.

2 What should a volunteer say to an inmate?
   a) Discuss his crime and how he feels about it.
   b) Discuss anything that relates to some common interest.
   c) Discuss biblical topics only.

3. What should be done if a local jail has no religious program?
   a) Complain to the sheriff.
   b) Propose a program to the head jailer.
   c) Seek other avenues of ministry to inmates.
   d) All of the above.
   e) b) and c).

4. A person who cannot actually visit in prisons or jails can
   a) pray for inmates, chaplains, and other volunteers.
   b) correspond with inmates.
   c) enlist others as volunteers.
   d) All of the above.

5. Single young women in prison programs can
   a) counsel youth and women inmates.
   b) concentrate on outside ministries.
   c) correspond with inmates.
   d) work as a member of a visitation team.
   e) All of the above.

6. What can pastors do to encourage congregations toward prison and jail ministries?
   a) Visit local jails and prisons to learn needs.
   b) Identify key church members who could direct the ministry.
   c) Preach sermons on this ministry.
   d) All of the above.

7. If an inmate appears to have emotional or other problems, the volunteer working with that inmate should
   a) attempt to present scriptural principles for dealing with those problems
   b) discuss the situation with the chaplain.
   c) recommend that the inmate seek professional counseling.

8. While working with inmates, a Christian volunteer should also be seeking ways to promote penal reform.
   a) True.
   b) False.

9. The most effective volunteers to minority-group prisoners are persons of that same minority group.
   a) Always true.
   b) Not always true.
   c) Never true.

10. Further information on prison and jail ministries is easily found from various books, magazines, and organizations.
    a) True.
    b) False.

11

To Learn More . . .

Don't stop now—you're just beginning.

This book is merely the first step, an introduction to learning how you can be Christ's ambassador to those behind bars. If you have read this far you are serious about considering prisons and jails as a place for ministry. Let me urge you to learn all you can. I have included some resources I think will give you a deeper understanding of the correctional system, and how you as a Christian volunteer can minister effectively within that system.

This chapter does not include every resource available, nor do I necessarily agree with all the viewpoints expressed in these materials. I simply want to give you some examples of what can be found if you are willing to look for it. Your church denomination may have its own materials for institutional ministries. Write to the headquarters and ask. A few prisons have prepared booklets for volunteers. If you happen to live near a prison or penitentiary, call or write the chaplain's office or the public information office. Check your local library for appropriate books and magazine articles; the librarian will be glad to help you find these. If there is a ministerial association in your community, call and ask what program they have for prison or jail ministries. Don't forget to inquire of your pastor and members of your church. You might be surprised to find others who are already involved in this way.

Don't hesitate to write to the organizations I have listed. They can direct you to other resources and programs for inmates.

Books

The Holy Bible. Start with your Bible and see what it says about prisons, prisoners, and the response of believers. Consider chapters like Genesis 39; Matthew 25; Acts 12, 16, 23; 1 Timothy 1; and others. Reflect on what God's Word says—and says *to you*.

Brodsky, Stanley L. *Families and Friends of Men in Prison.* Lexington, Mass.: D.C. Heath, 1975. Based on a detailed study of inmates and their families at the Illinois State Penitentiary. Documents the importance to inmates of correspondence and visitation.

Carter, Robert; Glaser, Daniel; and Wilkins, Leslie. *Correctional Institutions.* New York: Lippincott, 1977, 2nd ed. Basic textbook on prisons, jails, and the correctional system.

Chaplain/Volunteer Study Report. Canadian Penitentiary Service, Chaplaincy Division, 1975. A report on the use of volunteers in religious programs in Canadian prisons.

Garmon, William S. *Who Are the Criminals?* Nashville: Broadman Press, 1968. From a Christian perspective.

Glaser, Daniel, ed. *Handbook of Criminology.* New York: Random House, 1974. Basic resource book.

Goldfarb, Ronald. *Jails.* New York: Anchor Press/Doubleday, 1975. Extensive but readable discussion of local jails, with chapters on the situations of the mentally and physically ill, narcotics addicts, alcoholics, and juveniles.

The Jail: Its Operation and Management. Nick Pappas, ed., Washington, D.C.: U.S. Bureau of Prisons, n.d. (ca. 1971). Written for jail administrators but gives insight into problems of jails and the potential for volunteer programs.

Jogensen, James D. and Scheier, Ivan H. *Volunteer Training for Courts and Corrections.* Metuchen, N.J.: Scarecrow Press, 1973. For general volunteer involvement but adaptable to prison religious programs.

Kandle, George C. and Cassler, Henry H. *Ministering to Prisoners and Their Families*. New York: Prentice Hall, 1968. Directed to pastors (but useful for lay volunteers) to help counsel and assist prisoners and their families. Both authors have served as prison chaplains.

Mission Action Group Guide: Juvenile Rehabilitation. Birmingham, Ala.: Woman's Missionary Union, Southern Baptist Convention, 1967. Study guide for church groups concerned for rehabilitation of juvenile offenders.

Mission Action Group Guide: Prisoner Rehabilitation. Memphis: Brotherhood Commission, Southern Baptist Convention, 1968. Comprehensive study guide for church groups.

Pace, Dale K. *A Christian's Guide to Effective Jail & Prison Ministries.* Old Tappan, N.J.: Revell, 1976. Oriented to chaplains but valuable for volunteers. Gives an overview of the potential for Christian ministries plus specific guidelines for programs. Includes bibliography and directory of Christian organizations in prison ministries.

Richmond, Mark S. *Prison Profiles.* Dobbs Ferry, N.Y.: Oceana Publications, 1965. Describes many facets of the correctional system, based on author's twenty-five years of work in corrections. One chapter on the role of the chaplaincy.

Scheier, Iven H., *et al. Guidelines and standards for the use of volunteers in correctional programs.* Washington, D.C.: Law Enforcement Assistance Administration, 1972. Secular perspective but adaptable.

Studt, Elliot. *The Re-entry of the Offender into the Community.* Department of Health, Education & Welfare. Washington, D.C.: U.S. GPO, 1967. Looks at a critical period for offenders.

Magazines

Anderson, George M. "Jails, Lockups and Houses of Detention," *America*, January 10, 1976. Focuses on larger jails and detention facilities, based on author's service as chaplain at Rikers House of Detention, New York.

Axilbund, Melvin T. "American Prisons and Jails," *Current History*, June, 1976. Summary and descriptive background information on the U.S. correctional system, with all the basic statistics.

Doyle, Barrie. "Prison Ministry: Jesus in Jail," *Christianity Today*, July 5, 1974. Describes prison programs of two evangelical organizations.

Corrections Magazine. Non-technical articles on corrections.

Home Missions. Southern Baptist Convention, Home Mission Board. November, 1972. This issue devoted to Christian ministries in correctional institutions.

Spoelstra, Watson. "God Turns Prisons Inside Out," *Christian Life*, September, 1977. A look at the prison ministry of an ex-convict.

Films

The One-Way Door. Corrie ten Boom describes her concentration camp experiences and shows how God's love reaches into the worst of prisons. Available from World Wide Pictures, 1201 Hennepin Avenue South, Minneapolis, Minn. 55403. (No fee to prison chaplains.)

Set Free. Shows the ministry of Christian Ministries, 925 Sherlock Drive, Burbank, Calif. 91501. (No fee to prison chaplains).

Write to the Federal Bureau of Prisons, Washington, D.C. 20017, and ask for a list of available films.

Organizations

American Catholic Correctional Chaplains' Association, c/o Chaplain O'Brien, P.O. Box 32, Huntsville, Tex. 77340.

American Correctional Chaplains' Association, Woodridge Station, P.O. Box 10176, Washington, D.C.

American Protestant Correctional Chaplains' Association, c/o Rev. Adlai Lucas, Secretary-Treasurer, South Carolina Department of Corrections, P.O. Box 11159, Columbia, S.C. 29211.

Association of Christian Prison Workers, P.O. Box 2110, Orange, Calif. 92669.

Association of Evangelical Institutional Chaplains, 1036 South Highland Street, Arlington, Va. 22204.

Christian Prison Volunteers, Box 1949, Hollywood, Calif. 90028.

(For an extensive list of organizations, see Dale Pace, *A Christian's Guide to Effective Jail & Prison Ministries* (listed above), or the July, 1976 issue of the *Journal of the Association of Evangelical Institutional Chaplains*.)

Appendix

Instructor's Guidelines
Prison Volunteer Orientation Seminar

A prison-volunteer orientation seminar acquaints lay Christians with what is involved in jail and prison ministries. Not only does it describe the potential for such ministries, but also it provides an opportunity for personal evaluation concerning this type of ministry.

By attending such a seminar, many Christians will be challenged to commit themselves to an established prison ministry or will be encouraged to contact a chaplain who can provide more advanced or on-the-job training. The tangible result of this seminar will be increased numbers of Christians who are in some way ministering to and caring for inmates, former inmates, or families of inmates.

This appendix provides an overview of such a seminar and gives details on the mechanics of preparing and conducting one. Also included are examples of survey and evaluation forms that can be used during the seminar. You should feel free to use these examples when drawing up your own forms. The very act of having to respond to questions will prompt many to action.

COURSE CONTENT OUTLINE

The following is a general outline of the seminar course. Details of the presentation should come from the main text of this book, other materials, and the instructor's experience.

I. What is a prison and jail ministry?
   A. The nature of correctional institutions
      1. Numbers and types of institutions, inmates
      2. Distinction between "jail" and "prison"
      3. Functions: punishment, deterrent, rehabilitation
      4. Degree of success in each function: recidivism
      5. Ways prison, jails, and offenders affect other citizens
   B. The characteristics of inmates
      1. Typical inmate
      2. Inmates as individuals
      3. Christian inmates
   C. Daily life in prison or jail

II. Opportunities for ministry
   A. Inside
      1. Types of ministries: visitation, group activities, one-to-one, literature; short-term, long-term
      2. The role of the chaplain
      3. Relating to inmates as individuals
      4. When an inmate is approachable
      5. Ministering to the institution's staff

6. Basic rules for working in a jail or prison
7. How to teach and "preach"
8. How to lead a group Bible study
9. How to give a testimony
10. How to present a musical ministry

B. Outside
1. Correspondence
2. Caring for families
3. Sponsoring parolees/probationers
4. Counseling
5. Pre-trial intervention

III. Is prison ministry for you?
A. The Scriptural basis for prison ministry
B. Why become involved; the benefits
C. Types of people who should *not* be in prison work
D. Relating to chaplains
E. Personal preparation

IV. Qualities of an effective volunteer (During this segment, use the self-evaluation form and the local community pre-survey.)

PLANNING YOUR SEMINAR

If you have already taken part in planning and organizing a conference, seminar, or workshop, you know many of the tasks involved. If you have never had to organize such an event, don't be unduly concerned; it need not be difficult. In either case, the checklists, worksheets, and samples provided here will make your job easier.

Start thinking now about who can help you organize the seminar. One person may be able to help with many aspects of it; another may be able to work only on a single portion. Both kinds of people are needed.

Think of your seminar as a process that begins long before the participants come together and continues long after they have departed. Your planning should encompass this entire period.

Objectives

Begin planning by defining your objectives. What do you want to achieve as a result of this event and what do you want the participants to achieve? Ask yourself how the participants should be different when they leave the seminar. How should their attitudes be changed to encourage them toward jail and prison ministries? What misconceptions need to be corrected? What follow-up will reinforce the lessons of the seminar? Ideally, what are some things relating to prison ministries that participants should be doing three to six months after the seminar?

Below are possible objectives for the seminar; you may want to redefine these for your specific situation:

- Increase awareness of the potential for prison ministries
- Increase knowledge of prison and jail conditions
- Provide the biblical basis for prison ministry
- Describe specific forms of prison ministry and generally how to carry them out
- Provide a basis for self-evaluation concerning involvement
- Reinforce positive attitudes about prison ministries; counteract negative attitudes about jails and prisons
- Provide resources for further information

With your objectives in mind, you can arrange the content and presentation of the seminar to achieve those objectives. You might also want to project what portion (say, one fourth) of the participants will be involved in some form of prison ministry within six months after the seminar.

People, Place, and Time

Because they are so closely related, participants, meeting place, and date should be considered together.

Participants: Whom do you want to attend the seminar? Why? How many *could* attend from your area? How many are *likely* to attend? The estimated attendance will influence the selection of the meeting site.

Site: The seminar site must be carefully selected. If you have a variety of places to choose from, consider such things as accessibility (How easy is it to find? Is there adequate parking?), atmosphere (a motel meeting room, a church basement, a school classroom) and seating (Are seats fixed or movable, metal or padded? Will there be enough room?). These elements will influence the way the participants feel about the seminar and the way they respond to its content. Consider, too, the acoustics of the meeting place and the availability of a public address system. No site will have everything, but use the checklist in this section to help you find and analyze a suitable meeting place.

Date: The date of the seminar may be determined by elements beyond your control, such as site availability; but whenever possible, consider potential conflicts that would affect your desired audience. Set the date far enough ahead to give you enough time to prepare adequately and to inform possible participants.

Agenda

The seminar will typically require six to eight hours to present, but this time can be arranged in a variety of ways (see sample schedules). Allow time for breaks and perhaps a meal (which could be "brown bagged," catered, or served cafeteria-style, depending on the local situation).

The suggested schedules on page 127ff. are designed to cover the key material but are flexible enough to permit use of films, guest speakers, small discussion groups, or role-playing activities. There may be "slippage" so don't try to cram too much into the time available. Be sure guest speakers know when they are to speak well in advance of the seminar, and then send a reminder just before the seminar date.

Involve the audience in the program whenever possible. At appropriate intervals ask for their ideas or comments, and build on them. At the start, call for a show of hands of those who have already had some involvement in a prison ministry. You won't be able to change significantly the content of the seminar at this point, but you may be able to eliminate or expand certain segments depending on the audience's awareness. End the seminar with practical suggestions. Show how and what can be done. Begin the seminar crisply with a welcoming introduction, and bring it to an end with a positive, clear conclusion.

Organization

Don't try to do everything yourself. Get one or more persons to assist you. Delegate responsibilities and assign deadlines. Keep a list of who is doing what, and periodically check on each volunteer's progress. Logical areas of responsibility are (1) site selection and preparation, (2) participant invitation and registration, and (3) materials and equipment. Have several people assist you on the day of the seminar and know who is the key contact at the meeting site.

Participant Materials

If you are using this book as a resource, order enough copies well in advance. You may also want to use handouts of the seminar outline, leaving room for notes, resource lists, and descriptions of local ministries. Determine the quantities you'll need and arrange for ordering or reproduction. Decide how and where to distribute the handout materials. In some situations it may be possible to have displays or book tables. The key is to know what you want, order it in plenty of time, and have someone responsible for keeping track of materials at the seminar.

Support Materials and Equipment

Decide if you will need a public address system, films, or other audio-visual items (overhead projector, cassette recorder, etc.). Arrange for equipment well in advance of the seminar, and be sure the audience will be able to see or hear whatever is used. Audio-visual equipment will work well *if* carefully tested in advance. Don't assume that things will work automatically when the switch is thrown. Have someone check all plugs and wiring connections and actually turn on and test everything before the meeting. Plan for such things as extension cords, extra projector bulbs, and spare film reels. If you will need to speak from notes in a darkened room, have a podium light, small spotlight, or flashlight available.

Funding

Whether you charge for participation in the seminar may depend on your situation, but there are costs involved. Remember, most people appreciate what they pay for more than what they get for free. You may want to charge just the cost of this book, or you may want and need to include other seminar costs as well (postage, printing and photocopying, film or equipment rental, room rental, and refreshments). In some situations, the seminar sponsor may be able to find some way to underwrite all or most of the costs involved.

If participants are to pay, the money may be requested in advance with a registration form; or registration and fees may be collected at the door. In either case, have a simple means to record the funds received and to provide receipts if requested.

If you want some person or group to underwrite the seminar, you will need a presentation, probably in writing, in which you clearly describe the purpose of the seminar, its desired results and benefits, and exactly what costs will be incurred. The presentation need not be formal or lengthy, but it must show why you need the funds and how they are to be used.

Publicity

You will need to publicize the seminar well in advance and through several channels. Invitations should be sent to all area churches. Design and print flyers that can be included with the invitations. A letter and flyer may also be sent to local newspapers and radio and TV stations. Agencies that would like to know of the seminar include government offices concerned with offenders and corrections and certain social service agencies. You may also know of some individuals who are interested in prison and jail ministries; be sure to invite them. The important thing is to get the word out early and widely.

Evaluation and Follow-up

The conference isn't over when the participants leave. A follow-up plan is essential. A letter or telephone call within three weeks of the seminar to thank people for their participation, encourage their interest in prisons and jails, and remind them that you have resources to offer them could be the extra impetus needed for those considering personal involvement in a prison ministry.

If you are able to do a more extensive follow-up, you may want to send a simple postcard or single-sheet survey about sixty to ninety days after the seminar. The purpose of this survey would be to find out what lasting impact the seminar had as well as to further remind the participants about the importance of this ministry. The results of such a survey would also be useful to you in planning a similar seminar in the future.

For immediate evaluation, you should devise a simple form for participants to complete at the end of the seminar. This will help you determine the weaknesses and strengths of each segment of the seminar. Improvement can then be made in future seminars.

SEMINAR PLANNING SCHEDULE

This checklist suggests the timing when various general tasks must be accomplished for a smoothly run seminar. Use the Seminar and Facilities Checklist for details.

Up to Sixty Days Prior to Seminar

1. Meeting site selected.
2. Date selected.
3. Participant groups identified, attendance estimated.
4. Guest speaker(s) identified, contacted.

Thirty to Sixty Days Prior

1. Publicity prepared, first invitations sent.
2. Films ordered.
3. Agenda confirmed.
4. Responsibilities assigned to volunteers.

Fifteen to Thirty Days Prior

1. Meeting site evaluated.
2. Additional publicity released.
3. Food arrangements confirmed.
4. Handout materials being prepared; begin reproduction.
5. Arrange overnight accommodations.

One to Seven Days Prior

1. Confirm all arrangements.
2. Arrange transportation.
3. Gather and test audio-visual equipment (on site if possible).
4. Set up registration table the night before.

Seminar Day

1. Have all volunteers on hand and aware of duties.
2. Set up book table or displays.
3. Test public address system just prior to meeting.
4. Insure all equipment and aids are on hand.
5. Check heating/air conditioning.
6. Bring all handout materials.
7. Confirm food arrangements.

Up to Seven Days After

1. Send "thank you's."
2. Review evaluation forms.
3. Return all borrowed items.

Seven to Thirty Days After

1. Complete all financial accounting.

Sixty to Ninety Days After

1. Conduct follow-up postcard/letter survey.

Appendix

SAMPLE SEMINAR AND FACILITIES CHECKLIST

This checklist covers many aspects of seminars in different settings. Not all of the items will apply to your situation. Check off the items as completed. Place an X if the item is not applicable. Review the checklist regularly for items still blank. Assign major pending tasks to volunteers, and give them a date by which the task should be completed.

	Check off as completed or verified. X=not applicable
Planning	
1. Seminar objectives established.	____
2. Possible meeting places identified.	____
3. Tentative dates chosen.	____
4. Potential participants (or groups) identified	____
5. Potential attendance estimated. (How many?___)	____
6. Tentative agenda prepared.	____
7. Cooperative organizations identified.	____
8. Tentative budget prepared.	____
9. Volunteer help identified.	____
Site	
1. Meeting site available on desired date.	____
2. Adequate parking available.	____
3. Building or room to be unlocked (who has key?).	____
4. Contact person at site ________________.	____
5. Barrier-free access for wheelchair participants.	____
Meeting Room	
1. Room large enough for estimated attendance.	____
2. Speaker's platform visible from all parts of room.	____
3. Heating/air conditioning adequate.	____
4. Entrance for latecomers at rear (if possible).	____
5. Room located far from street or other noise source.	____
6. Lectern or table available for speaker (lighted?).	____
7. Enough chairs available.	____
8. Space inside or outside for coffee breaks.	____
9. Space for registration table.	____
10. Space for book table or displays.	____
11. Adequate lighting.	____
12. Lighting controls located.	____
13. Electrical outlets near A-V equipment.	____
Audio-visual Facilities	
1. Public address system available and working.	____
2. Someone available to test and control sound system.	____

3. Stand-up or lapel mikes needed, available. ___
4. Motion-picture projector needed, available. ___
5. Slide projector needed, available. ___
6. Screen (or white wall) available. ___
7. Screen visible from all parts of room. ___
8. Extension cords available. ___
9. Remote control for slide projector. ___
10. Extra bulbs for projectors. ___
11. Three-prong plug adapter. ___
12. Blackboard (chalk, erasers). ___
13. Paper pad easel (marking pens, pointer). ___
14. Other A-V equipment, materials __________ ___
15. Films ordered. ___
16. Films on hand. ___

Luncheon (if applicable)

1. Seating and table arrangements determined. ___
2. Adequate tables available. ___
3. Food preparations arranged. ___
4. Clean-up and serving arranged. ___
5. Adequate trash containers. ___

Coffee Breaks

1. Refreshments arrangements made. ___
2. Adequate tables for food, drink items. ___

Agenda

1. Agenda confirmed. ___
2. Agenda communicated to all involved. ___
3. Guest speakers confirmed. ___

Transportation

1. Arranged for incoming guest speaker(s). ___
2. Overnight accommodations arranged. ___

Registration

1. Pre-registration forms prepared. ___
2. Invitations sent. ___
3. Signs for meeting placed (walls, room door, building announcement board, etc.) ___
4. Table(s) available for registration. ___
5. Person(s) designated to run registration. ___
6. Cash boxes needed. ___
7. Receipt books needed. ___
8. Name tags needed, available (pens, pins). ___
9. Handout materials at registration table. ___

Participant Materials

1. Handout materials (book, outline, etc.) determined. ____
2. Preparation of in-house materials assigned. ____
3. Materials ordered. (How many copies?____) ____
4. Materials received. ____
5. Person assigned to bring materials to meeting. ____
6. Manner of distribution decided (before, during, after seminar). ____
7. Person assigned to pass out materials. ____
8. Preliminary survey reproduced. ____
9. Seminar evaluation form reproduced. ____

Publicity

1. Invitation letters sent. ____
2. Bulletin board flyers distributed. ____
3. News release or flyer sent to media. ____

Evaluation and Follow-up

1. Instructor's evaluation for personal reference. ____
2. "Thank you" call or letter to:
   - key participants or groups ____
   - guest speakers ____
   - meeting site host ____
3. Seminar evaluation forms reviewed. ____
4. Post-card survey (60-90 days later). ____

Administration

1. Billing arrangements for meals, rooms, equipment, etc. ____
2. Travel vouchers obtained. ____
3. Requisitions, purchase orders obtained. ____
4. Coordination with appropriate lateral or higher-level offices. ____

POSSIBLE SEMINAR SCHEDULES

One-day seminar

8:30 A.M.	Registration
9–9:10	Introduction
9:10–10:30	What's prison ministry all about? (possible film)
10:30–10:45	Break
10:45–11:45	Opportunities and alternatives
11:45–12:00	Question and answer
12:00–12:45 P.M.	Lunch
12:45–3:00 (or 4:00)	Is it for you? (possible film)
3:00–3:30 (or 4:00–4:30)	Question and answer; evaluation; conclusion

Day and a half

Day 1	7–9:30 P.M.	What's prison ministry all about?
Day 2	9–10:30	Opportunities and alternatives
	10:30–10:45	Break
	10:45–12:00	Is it for you?
		Question and answer
		Evaluation (or into mid-afternoon)
		Conclusion

Three evenings

Day 1 What's prison ministry all about?
Day 2 Opportunities and alternatives.
Day 3 Is it for you? Evaluation. Conclusion.

SAMPLE PRELIMINARY SURVEY FORM
Jail and Prison Ministries

in ______________________________
(your community)

Complete these questions to the best of your knowledge. When you return to your community, make telephone calls or visits to complete and revise the information. This will help you in your thinking about the potential for a prison or jail ministry in your community.

1. Which of the following correctional institutions are found in or near your community: (check all that apply)

Correctional Institutions in My Community	Yes	No	Don't know
county/city jail			
state prison			
federal prison/correctional institute			
boys'/girls' reformatory			
work or road camp, farm			
halfway house/work release center			
other:			

2. Which of the above institutions has some form of regular religious activity (worship service, Bible study, etc.)?

____ ( ) Don't know

3. Of the institutions which do not seem to have regular religious activities, which one is most likely to be open to the possibility of having such activity?
________________________________ ( ) Don't know

4. In my community, the most needed form of prison/jail ministry is probably
________________________________.

5. To contact the chaplain, warden, or administrator of one of these institutions or someone in a criminal offender or pre-trial intervention program, the first place I'd look for a telephone number or address is ________________; the second place is ________________.

SAMPLE SELF-EVALUATION FORM

Complete this form for yourself during the seminar. Keep it and review it after you return to your home community.

1. After what has been presented in the seminar so far, what do you think is the greatest need of most jail or prison inmates, their families, or of ex-offenders?

2. Of the different kinds of ministries and programs described, which one or two seem to you to be especially effective?

3. If the opportunity came along and you had the time to serve, which type of prison or jail ministry would you prefer?

4. About what do you feel most uncertain or uncomfortable when thinking about a personal involvement in a prison or jail ministry?

Look at this form later. Begin to pray about your answer to question 4, then to question 3. Be open to God's direction in your life about prison and jail ministries.

Notes

Chapter 1

1. Melvin T. Axilbund, "American Prisons and Jails," *Current History* (June 1976), p. 268.
2. *Ibid.*, pp. 266-67.
3. Ronald Goldfarb, *Jails: The Ultimate Ghetto* (New York: Anchor Press, 1975).
4. "U.S. Prison Population Again Hits New High," *Corrections Magazine* (March 1972).
5. The most recent reported survey of local jails was done in 1972 by the Law Enforcement Assistance Administration. This survey reported 141,600 inmates, but many believe this total is low. *Sourcebook of Criminal Justice Statistics 1975*, U.S. National Criminal Justice Information and Statistics Service (Washington, D.C.: U.S. GPO, 1976).
6. *Corrections Magazine* (March 1977).
7. Hans W. Mattick, "The Contemporary Jails of the United States," in Daniel Glaser, ed., *Handbook of Criminology* (New York: Random House, 1974), p. 777.
8. Goldfarb, *Jails*.
9. "Family Visiting at San Quentin," *Corrections Magazine* (July-August 1975).
10. Dale K. Pace, *A Christian's Guide to Effective Jail & Prison Ministries* (Old Tappan, N.J.: Revell, 1976), pp. 83-84.
11. President's Commission on Law Enforcement and Administration of Justice, *Task Force Report: Corrections* (Washington, D.C.: U.S. GPO, 1967).
12. Axilbund, "American Prisons," p. 268.
13. F. P. Scioli and T. J. Cook, "How Effective Are Volunteers?" *Crime and Delinquency*, vol. 22, no. 2 (1976) (abstract).
14. Paul R. Markstrom, *Volunteers in Corrections Manual* (1977), pp. 26-28.

Chapter 2

1. "What God is Doing at Leavenworth Penitentiary," *Pentecostal Evangel*, November 9, 1975, p. 11.
2. *Ibid.*, p. 18.

Chapter 3

1. Axilbund, "American Prisons," pp. 266-67.
2. From *Ibid.* Also Leonard Orland, *Prisons: Houses of Darkness* (New York: Free Press, 1975); *Corrections Magazine* (March 1977).
3. Axilbund, "American Prisons." Quoted from Bureau of Census, *1970 Census of Population, Subject Report: Persons in Institutions and Other Group Quarters.*
4. *The Challenge of Crime in a Free Society* (Washington, D.C.: U.S. GPO, 1967), p. 44.
5. *Training Manual for Volunteers*, Yokefellow Prison Ministry of North Carolina (1976), p. 13.
6. Frederick R. Silber, "Yokefellow in the Prison Setting" mimeographed (n.d.).
7. *Chaplain/Volunteer Study Report*, Canadian Penitentiary Service, Chaplaincy Division (1975), p. 2.

Notes

Chapter 4

1. Law Enforcement Assistance Administration, "The Nation's Jails" (report of the 1972 survey), reprinted in Robert Carter, Daniel Glaser, and Leslie Wilkins, *Correctional Institutions*, 2nd ed. (New York: Lippincott, 1977).
2. Axilbund, "American Prisons."
3. "America's Jails: How Bad Are They?" *U.S. News & World Report*, June 23, 1975.
4. "Jails and Criminal Justice," *Prisoners in America* (1973).
5. Axilbund, "American Prisons."
6. Goldfarb, *Jails*.

Chapter 5

1. Pace, *A Christian's Guide*, p. 93.

Chapter 6

1. Quoted in Kevin Krajick, "Lifers Try to Scare the Crime Out of Juveniles," *Corrections Magazine* (December 1977), p. 19.
2. *The Jail: Its Operation and Management*, U.S. Bureau of Prisons (n.d.), p. 42.
3. *Prison Ministry Guide* (Jacksonville, Fla.: Florida Baptist Convention, n.d.), p. 3.
4. "The Gospel Behind Bars," *Newsweek*, March 29, 1976, pp. 84-85.

Chapter 7

1. Cited in *The Jail: Its Operation and Management*.
2. John M. Gandy, "Volunteers in four provincial adult correctional institutions: services provided and perceptions of inmates and staff," *Canadian Journal of Criminology and Corrections*, vol. 19, no. 1 (1977); abstracted in *Criminal Justice Abstracts* (June 1977), p. 177.
3. Markstrom, *Volunteers*, p. 11.
4. *Ibid.*
5. *Training Manual for Volunteers*.
6. Silber, "Yokefellow in the Prison Setting."
7. *Ibid.*
8. *Ibid.*

Chapter 8

1. *Mission Action Guide: Prisoner Rehabilitation*, Southern Baptist Convention (1968), p. 14.
2. Stanley L. Brodsky, *Families and Friends of Men in Prison* (Lexington, Mass.: DC Heath, 1975), p. 1.

Chapter 9

1. "Laymen Share Christ with Prison Inmates," *Prison Ministry Guide* (Jacksonville, Fla.: Florida Baptist Convention, n.d.).

Answers to Review Questions

Chapter 1	1. c	2. c	3. c	4. b	5. b	6. b	7. b	8. a	9. a	10. your choice
Chapter 2	1. a	2. c	3. b	4. a	5. f	6. b	7. a	8. d	9. b	10. b
Chapter 3	1. b	2. c	3. b	4. b	5. b	6. b	7. a	8. a	9. a	10. b
Chapter 4	1. b	2. a	3. b	4. d	5. a	6. b	7. a	8. b	9. b	10. a
Chapter 5	1. a	2. a	3. a	4. b	5. c	6. b	7. b	8. b	9. c	10. d
Chapter 6	1. b	2. b	3. a	4. a	5. c	6. d	7. e	8. a	9. b	10. b
Chapter 7	1. a	2. b	3. b	4. b	5. a	6. a	7. b	8. c	9. b	10. b
Chapter 8	1. a	2. a	3. b	4. d	5. b	6. a	7. a	8. b	9. b	10. c
Chapter 9	1. b	2. b	3. d	4. b	5. a	6. b	7. a	8. d	9. b	10. b
Chapter 10	1. a	2. b	3. e	4. d	5. e	6. d	7. b	8. b	9. b	10. a